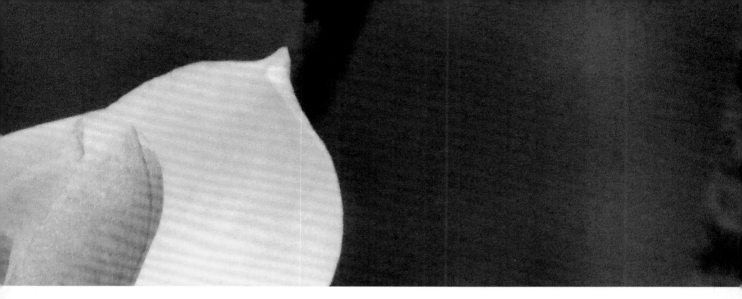

THE **PLANT LOVER'S GUIDE** TO
MA**GNOLIAS**

ANDREW BUNTING

TIMBER PRESS
PORTLAND, OREGON

CONTENTS

54
**146 Magnolias
for the Garden**

198
**Growing and
Propagating**

WHY I LOVE MAGNOLIAS

I spent my high school years in a split-level house in the south suburbs of Chicago, in a little town called Manhattan. Surrounded by mostly uninspiring plantings—a few ubiquitous elm trees, a blue spruce in the front yard, and a few bur oaks—it was there, almost by necessity, that I began to take a keen interest in gardening. My mother gave me full reign in the yard; she even let me install a fairly large vegetable garden out front, the only part of the yard that had sun—a first in this somewhat conservative midwestern community! I also started an annual garden both from seed and from plants I had grown under lights in the basement. Ageratums, cosmos, impatiens, and

A large saucer magnolia specimen growing at the edge of Swarthmore College near the Palmer dormitory.

marigolds were all easy to grow from seed. In the vegetable garden, I grew tomatoes, carrots, lettuce, radishes, and a bumper crop of cucumbers.

Furthering my plant obsession, my bedroom window sat literally in the canopy of an old majestic saucer magnolia, *Magnolia ×soulangeana*, that bloomed reliably and in profusion every spring. The tree was most likely planted when the house was built, so the branches engulfed the top and sides of the house. The windows in that bedroom provided a great vantage point for studying the magnolia. This tree in particular opened my eyes to the beauty of flowering trees.

My appreciation for magnolias certainly started there, but it only expanded as I learned more. In my college ornamental horticulture program I was required to complete two internships, one of which landed me at Morton Arboretum in Lisle, Illinois, and the other at Chicago Botanic Garden. Along with my coursework, these experiences opened my eyes to the wide variety of magnolias. Ray Schulenberg, then curator at Morton Arboretum, would take us on regular walks to show us the breadth of the collection, and Chicago housed a wide variety of trees. It was at Scott Arboretum of Swarthmore College, however, where I would work for 26 years, that my passion for the genus really exploded. Their collection of predominantly *M. ×soulangeana*, *M. kobus*, and *M. stellata* cultivars dates all the way back to the 1930s. And around the borough of Swarthmore, equally majestic specimens are easy to come by. I remember local plantsman Charles Cresson telling me about these specimens in the late 1980s, and they are only more impressive today. As curator at the arboretum, we built our collection from about 50 to 200 cultivars over a 20 year period.

When I joined the board of directors for the Magnolia Society International around 2008, I was surrounded with people who ate, drank, and slept magnolias. Spending time with experts like Richard Figlar, Larry Langford, Raymond Sutton, Kevin Parris, Phelan Bright, and others made my passion grow even stronger. Before this experience, I was not fully aware of the incredible diversity of magnolia cultivars, hybrids, and species, nor was I aware that magnolias are cultivated around the world as important ornamental plants. For years, I knew there were some magnolias native to the United States and many others

The heart of the Magnolia Collection at Scott Arboretum of Swarthmore College. Most of these specimens were planted in the early 1930s.

found throughout parts of Asia, but from my time with the Magnolia Society International, I have realized the global diversity of the species. Magnolias are found throughout the Caribbean, in Central and North America (with over 30 species in Mexico, alone), throughout all of southeastern Asia (with over 100 species in China), and in Thailand, Vietnam, Japan, Korea, and others.

Magnolias thrive outside of our gardens, too. Over the last several years, I have had many exciting opportunities to see native magnolias growing *in situ*. On a trip to Sichuan, China, in 2010, my colleagues and I saw beautiful specimens of *Magnolia sargentiana* and *M. dawsoniana*. Each was over 100 years old, if not older, and it was impressive to see them in such a mature state. In 2012 in Taiwan, we collected *M. compressa* and searched for the elusive southern species, *M. kachirachirai*. In 2013 in northern Vietnam, we saw several impressive trees, including *M. cathcartii*, *M. foveolata*, and the local endemic *M. sapaensis*. And in January of 2014, I joined several other board members from the Magnolia Society International on a trip to Colombia where we were hosted by fellow member Marcela Serna Gonzalez, who showed us many incredible wild populations of magnolias, including *M. hernandezii* and *M. jardinensis*, among others.

Magnolia dawsoniana, seen here at the National Trust garden, Lanhydrock in Cornwall, England.

Magnolia foveolata, seen here growing at Richard and Anita Figlar's home garden in Pickens, South Carolina.

Since joining the board of the Magnolia Society International, my knowledge and appreciation for the diversity of hybrids and cultivars, as well as naturally occurring species, has grown exponentially.

At home, at Scott Arboretum, and for my design and build company, Fine Garden Creations, I have taken full advantage of the wide-ranging roles magnolias can play in the garden and landscape. Depending on the cultivar or species, and the area of the world where you live, you can find a magnolia in flower every month of the year. In Cuba, the native magnolias start flowering in November. In Tallahassee, Florida, the earliest cultivars, such as *Magnolia zenii* 'Pink Parchment' and *M.* 'March Til Frost', start flowering in January. In the Mid-Atlantic states, the first magnolia to flower is the Yulan magnolia, *M. denudata*. The sweetbay magnolia, *M. virginiana* var. *australis*, can bloom from mid- to late spring in its native habitat.

They are versatile, too. While many magnolias prefer or need well-drained soils, there are some, like the umbrella magnolia, *Magnolia tripetala*, and *M. virginiana* var. *australis* that fulfill an important niche in the garden and can grow in very wet conditions. *Magnolia tripetala*, with its large, tropical foliage, can produce a stunning effect when planted alongside a stream.

There are many evergreen options, as well. For decades, the primary evergreen magnolia used was the southern magnolia, *Magnolia grandiflora*, but today many excellent selections exist, such as *M. doltsopa*, *M. insignis*, *M. yuyuanensis*, and *M. figo*, along with many hybrids. And the color range for flowers is quite impressive, including pure white, cream, sulfur yellow, golden yellow, pink, cerise, rose, purple, and now nearly red. Some plants are quite small and shrubby, like *M. virginiana* var. *australis* Sweet Thing 'Perry Paige', while others, like the cucumber tree, *M. acuminata*, can grow to be over 100 feet (30 m) tall.

Magnolia zenii 'Pink Parchment' blooming early at Pleasant Run Nursery in Allentown, New Jersey.

The evergreen *Magnolia insignis*, shown here in Richard and Anita Figlar's garden.

Magnolias have indeed been popular for centuries, but today they are experiencing quite a renaissance—perhaps more so than the genus has ever experienced before. New species are being discovered; there are many global conservation projects occurring to preserve magnolias in Cuba, Colombia, China, Mexico, Costa Rica, and the United States; and hybridizers are using the vast wealth of genetic material available to create magnolias that vaguely resemble traditional magnolias.

From childhood and throughout my youth and professional life, magnolias have been a steady presence. Undoubtedly, that massive saucer magnolia outside my window was the starting point, but even after all these years, my passion and excitement for the genus only seems to intensify. This book is my attempt to share that with you.

DESIGNING WITH MAGNOLIAS

A massive *Magnolia campbellii* specimen, seen here growing in England.

T

The thought of a magnolia in the landscape means many different things to gardeners across the globe. In April, one of the first magnolias to flower in the northeastern United States is that same plant from my youth, *Magnolia ×soulangeana*. If you could quantify it, there is no other spring-flowering tree that produces as much flowering year in and year out. As it begins to bloom in midspring, the naked branches are covered in large pink or white flowers. These are the most prolific flower colors among magnolias, but you can also find them in yellow, orange, red, and purple.

From Washington, DC, and into the Southeast, the large and stately southern magnolias, *Magnolia grandiflora*, are iconic. These large trees are found around many of the federal buildings throughout the capitol, including a pair planted by Andrew Jackson in 1830 at the South Portico to the White House, as well as others throughout the grounds planted by Franklin D. Roosevelt and Warren G. Harding. Throughout the South, the southern magnolia is ubiquitous and found in both residential and commercial plantings. Moore Farms Botanical Garden in South Carolina holds the North American Plant Collections Consortium's national collection of *M. grandiflora* cultivars. I have also seen large specimens of *M. grandiflora* planted in a hotel garden on the shores of Lake Como, Italy, and used as the primary street tree along the roads and avenues of Bogota, Colombia.

On the West Coast of the United States, magnolia species and cultivars not usually found in other parts of the country abound. The climate in San Francisco (Zone 10) is perfect for growing the highly coveted Campbell's magnolia, *Magnolia campbellii*, and at San Francisco Botanical Garden a large specimen of the evergreen *M. doltsopa* is a striking site in early spring. While the Midwest is far more limited in its choices, there are many magnolias with exceptional hardiness, such as the star magnolia, *M. stellata*, which is commonplace in many midwestern gardens. There are only a few magnolias native just west of the Mississippi River, but seven species are native east of the Mississippi, including *M. grandiflora*, *M. macrophylla*, and *M. tripetala*, among others.

In the United Kingdom and throughout Europe, magnolias are hallmarks of the early spring landscape, so much so that the Royal Horticultural Society (RHS) has given the Award of Garden Merit to 42 exceptional magnolias, including *Magnolia* 'Caerhays Belle', *M.* 'David Clulow', and *M.* ×*loebneri* 'Wildcat'. Caerhays Castle in southwestern England is home to a national magnolia collection that includes many of the finest specimens in England. In Belgium, Arboretum Wespelaar has one of the largest collections in the world and has produced many outstanding hybrids, including 'Daphne' and 'Anilou'.

In the Southern Hemisphere, magnolias are popular in Australia and New Zealand. Kiwi hybridizers Oz Blumhardt, Felix Jury, Mark Jury, and Vance Hooper have bred many outstanding cultivars, including several with nearly red flowers that thrive in both Australian and New Zealand gardens, as well as in many gardens in Zones 7 and up in the Northern Hemisphere.

While we revere magnolias for their exceptional flowering, many other attributes abound. Most cultivated magnolias are deciduous, but there are many beautiful evergreen species. A few have interesting variegated foliage, like *Magnolia virginiana* var. *australis* 'Mattie Mae Smith', and several of the North American species have oversized leaves that provide a tropical effect in the garden (for example, *M. tripetala* and *M. macrophylla* subsp. *ashei*). Most of the ornamental magnolias are more tree-like, but several, like *M. virginiana* var. *australis* Sweet Thing 'Perry Paige' and several cultivars of *M. laevifolia*, can be used as shrubs.

A beautiful specimen of *Magnolia stellata* 'Centennial' growing next to the historic Benjamin West House on the campus of Swarthmore College.

Magnolia 'Genie', a red introduction from New Zealander Vance Hooper, grows here at Pleasant Run Nursery in Allentown, New Jersey.

Ashe's magnolia, *Magnolia macrophylla* subsp. *ashei*, has bold, luxuriant, tropical foliage; shown here growing at Tower Hill Botanic Garden in Boylston, Massachusetts.

Magnolias can be used for screening, trimmed into topiary, or effectively displayed as an espalier on the side of a building. Some cultivars are diminutive and others have a very upright or fastigiate (branches point upward) habit, making them perfect for small spaces. *Magnolia* 'Genie' is a compact tree that stays under 15 feet (5 m), and 'Lilliputian' is a small cultivar of *M.* ×*soulangeana*.

Fragrance is as much a calling card of magnolias as the bountiful flowers: almost all of them have some fragrance, and in most cases it is exceptional (there are a few examples where the fragrance is off-putting, but these are very rare). The tropical *Magnolia champaca*, for instance, has a strong spicy fragrance. In many southeastern Asian countries it is common to see a small flower hanging from the visor in a taxi or in a small vase on the front desk of a hotel lobby to function as an air freshener. *Magnolia delavayi* is fragrant at night and *M.* 'Judy Zuk' has the fragrance of fruit.

Magnolia laevifolia 'Michelle' is a great evergreen magnolia that is perfect as a single specimen or for screening and hedging.

Three-Season Interest

While magnolias may be mostly known for their spring flowers, there are many options that offer interest throughout the year. If you so desire, you can have magnolias in flower from winter to fall.

WINTER

In many parts of the world, magnolias start blooming very early in the season. In climates where the average winter temperature never drops below 10°F (–12°C), it is not unusual to see magnolias flowering in midwinter. The shrubby *Magnolia laevifolia*, for instance, generally blooms in winter and includes cultivars such as 'Copperstop', 'Michelle', and 'Snowbird', among others. These small trees or large shrubs have rust-colored buds that open to reveal 4 inch (10 cm) white flowers with striking yellow stamens that are borne in profusion. *Magnolia doltsopa* is a strongly scented evergreen tree with white flowers that generally appear from midwinter to early spring. Other exceptional evergreen winter-flowering magnolias include the relatively unknown *M. maudiae* and *M. maudiae* var. *platypetala*, with very fragrant flowers contrasted by purple stamens. *Magnolia* 'March Til Frost', a relatively small tree, does as the name implies, flowering from late winter through midautumn with wine-red, goblet-shaped flowers covering the naked branches. A specimen at the University of Florida's North Florida Research and Education Center (Zone 8a) typically flowers in February. Both *M. salicifolia* and *M. zenii* are winter flowering depending on their location. At Scott Arboretum (Zone 7) both species tend to bloom in late March or sometimes even earlier (because they flower so early, they often run the risk of having their tepals damaged by cold weather and frosts).

EARLY SPRING

The early spring–flowering magnolias would be defined in the Philadelphia area (Zone 7) as those that flower between the 1st and 15th of April. For us, this is the best time in the magnolia season to see an abundance of flowers (though again, it is a time when blooms can be damaged by cold nights). In this region, "early spring," "midspring," and "late spring" all overlap, creating an extended magnolia flowering season from early April to mid-May (this is

Magnolia doltsopa is a beautiful evergreen magnolia that flowers from midwinter to early spring. Seen here at San Francisco Botanical Garden in California.

Two stunning specimens of the early spring–flowering saucer magnolia, *Magnolia ×soulangeana*, grow in front of Swarthmore College's Wharton Dormitory.

in fact true of most regions, though the dates will obviously differ). At Scott Arboretum, early April brings an incredible show of saucer magnolia (*Magnolia ×soulangeana*) cultivars, almost all of which are exceptional. There are dozens of magnificent specimens festooned with pinkish white flowers. Outside of the gothic-style Wharton Dormitory there is a pair that grace the entrance that are close to 50 feet (15 m) tall with a nearly equal spread, and throughout the borough of Swarthmore, seemingly every old house has a magnificent specimen in the front yard.

For smaller gardens that might not be able to accommodate a saucer magnolia, both the star magnolia, *Magnolia stellata*, and the Loebner magnolia, *M. ×loebneri*, are excellent choices that offer abundant spring color. Depending on the cultivar, these are typically large, rounded shrubs to small, upright, oval-shaped trees. They have smaller and narrower tepals than the saucer magnolias and each flower often has dozens of tepals, creating a chrysanthemumlike effect. Both of these are also very hardy. *Magnolia stellata* 'Centennial' has white flowers and is an upright tree reaching approximately 20 feet (6 m) tall. 'Chrysanthemumiflora' is a many-tepaled pink clone. Combining attributes of both parents—the height of *M. kobus* with the compactness and fragrance of *M. stellata*—most

Magnolias for Early-Spring Flowering

Magnolia 'Athene' and 'Black Tulip'
Magnolia denudata and cultivars
Magnolia doltsopa
Magnolia 'Ivory Chalice'
Magnolia ×*kewensis* 'Wada's Memory'
Magnolia laevifolia and cultivars
Magnolia ×*loebneri* and cultivars
Magnolia salicifolia
Magnolia sargentiana var. *robusta*
Magnolia ×*soulangeana* and cultivars
Magnolia sprengeri var. *diva* 'Diva'
Magnolia stellata and cultivars

The popular *Magnolia* ×*loebneri* 'Leonard Messel' is a mainstay in the early spring garden throughout the East Coast and many midwestern states.

Magnolia denudata is one of the earliest of the spring-flowering magnolias.

Beautifully pyramidal in youth, *Magnolia* ×*kewensis* 'Wada's Memory' will broaden in stature over time. This young specimen is growing at Pleasant Run Nursery in Allentown, New Jersey.

of the *M.* ×*loebneri* cultivars are exceptional. 'Leonard Messel' is very popular—one of the nation's bestselling cultivars—with soft pink flowers and reaching only 15–20 feet (5–6 m) at maturity. 'Merrill', with white flowers, and 'Wildcat', with soft pink flowers, are also great choices.

There are many other spectacular trees for this time of year. One of the earliest trees to flower in Swarthmore is the upright Yulan magnolia, *Magnolia denudata*. We have also selected a clone with a fastigiate habit called 'Swarthmore Sentinel'. *Magnolia* 'Ivory Chalice' is a hybrid, but looks very much like the Yulan and has great hardiness. *Magnolia dawsoniana* reaches 30 feet (9 m) tall with large white flowers suffused with pink. Even earlier flowering than *M. denudata* is the anise magnolia, *M. salicifolia*, with pure white flowers emerging in early spring. At maturity the habit will be broadly pyramidal with a height and spread of 40 feet (12 m). An incredibly floriferous tree with strikingly beautiful pink flowers, *M. sprengeri* var. *diva* 'Diva' is a real gem in the garden. Another stunning tree is *M.* ×*kewensis* 'Wada's Memory'. It is fast growing with an upright broadly spire shape when young, but over time it broadens significantly. The long white tepals create wide starlike flowers on naked branches. New Zealander Felix Jury's soft pink *M.* 'Athene' and his son Mark Jury's diminutive *M.* 'Black Tulip' flower during this period, as well.

MIDSPRING

Midspring is usually when you'll find many (if not most) of the yellow-flowering magnolias in bloom. The typical parents of the yellows are the early-flowering *Magnolia denudata* and the much later-flowering cucumber tree, *M. acuminata*. Choice cultivars include 'Butterflies', 'Daphne', 'Elizabeth', 'Gold Star', 'Golden Gift', 'Lois', 'Sun Spire', 'Sunburst', 'Sunsation', 'Yellow Bird', and 'Yellow Lantern'. Many of the yellow-flowering magnolias are of very large stature, though two cultivars, 'Lois' and 'Golden Gift', are smaller and work well in gardens with less space or those in an urban environment.

Also smaller in stature, another group of magnolias that are great for this time of year are those that are often referred to as The Girls. These include 'Ann', 'Betty', 'Jane', and 'Susan', among others. They were introduced by the National Arboretum in 1962 and are typically hybrids of *Magnolia liliiflora* 'Nigra' and *M. stellata* 'Rosea'. The group ranges in color from pink to pinkish purple and typically blooms later and therefore is less likely to be frosted. Plants have a smaller and more shrublike stature.

Magnolias for Midspring Flowering

The Girls series
Magnolia ×*brooklynensis* and cultivars
Magnolia 'Butterflies'
Magnolia 'Elizabeth'
Magnolia 'Lois'
Magnolia macrophylla
Magnolia sieboldii
Magnolia tripetala
Magnolia virginiana var. *australis* and cultivars
Magnolia virginiana var. *virginiana* and cultivars

Magnolia 'Yellow Bird' is one of the last to flower of all the yellow magnolias.

Magnolia 'Ann', one of The Girls, blooms after the chance of frost has passed.

A fantastic, mature (over 50 years old) specimen of Magnolia 'Betty' at Scott Arboretum.

Magnolia 'Golden Gift' is a great yellow-flowering magnolia.

Magnolia fraseri is a North American native with large and almost tropical-looking leaves.

Magnolia ×brooklynensis 'Eva Maria' has a suffusion of yellow and pink in its flowers.

Two midspring-flowering Asian species, *Magnolia wilsonii* and *M. sieboldii*, are also shrublike. Over time these will become large and broad statured. Both are characterized by having flower buds that look like pendant eggs. The pure white flowers open to reveal a contrast between the alabaster white tepals and a boss (swelling) of deep, dark purple stamens. The flowers of *M. sieboldii* are more pendant. I have seen this species planted atop a wall or on a bank where passersby can walk under the arching branches. The flowers on *M. wilsonii* vary from pendant to outward facing.

Several of the large-leaved North American species blooming midspring include *Magnolia macrophylla*, *M. tripetala*, *M. fraseri*, and *M. macrophylla* subsp. *ashei*, Ashe's magnolia. While these are all stunning plants with luxuriant tropical foliage, they will require a reasonable amount of space. Ashe's magnolia, which still has the bold attributes but only reaches 20 feet (6 m) tall at maturity, is an exception and is perfect for smaller suburban gardens.

Magnolia virginiana var. *australis* 'Mattie Mae Smith' is an evergreen sweetbay with beautifully variegated leaves of yellow and green.

Created at Brooklyn Botanic Garden, *Magnolia* ×*brooklynensis* is a cross between *M. acuminata* and *M. liliiflora*, and retains the later flowering from both parents with a suffusion of pink or purple flowers from *M. liliiflora* with the yellows of *M. acuminata*. Cultivars include 'Hattie Carthan', 'Eva Maria', and 'Woodsman'.

Famed Wisconsin plant hybridizer Dennis Ledvina has bred many cultivars of magnolias to thrive in colder regions. These include magnolias that will flower later and thus not run the risk of being affected by the colder temperatures of early spring. His 'Blushing Belle', a hybrid between 'Yellow Bird' and 'Caerhays Belle', is a large-flowered pink magnolia with many of the attributes of 'Caerhays Belle', but much more cold hardy, to –20°F (–29°C). 'Red Baron' has large, deep rose-red flowers with white interiors. It is the resulting cross between *M. acuminata* and 'Big Dude'. 'Silk Road' has large upward-facing, late-flowering white flowers like one of its parents, *M. tripetala*. 'Rose Marie' is a pyramidal tree with pink flowers and a hybrid between 'Pink Surprise' and 'Daybreak'.

Flowering in the later part of the midspring season are the sweetbay magnolias, *Magnolia virginiana* var. *australis* and *M. virginiana* var. *virginiana*. These both produce small creamy white flowers that are borne sporadically through the tree and start to appear in late spring in Zone 7, continuing until early autumn. While the flowers don't cover the tree like on some of the earlier-flowering magnolias, the scent is so enticing that it will more than make up for it; plant sweetbay magnolias near a threshold or next to an entrance or a patio so that the smells can be regularly enjoyed. Variety *australis* is more treelike. Depending on the clone and winter temperatures, it might be evergreen, semi-evergreen, or deciduous in moderate regions. Variety *virginiana* is more thicket forming and will be deciduous. Because of its tolerance of moisture, it is versatile in the garden. It very much lends itself to naturalistic plantings in areas that might have drainage issues. That said, it can also make a beautiful specimen tree. At The Scott Arboretum, 'Henry Hicks' is planted as the focal point in two different courtyards, 'Satellite' is a strong evergreen anchor of the corner of a building, and 'Santa Rosa' creates shade in a sunny courtyard. At a friend's garden in Wilmington, Delaware (Zone 7a), 'Mattie Mae Smith' brightens a shady area with its yellow-and-green variegated leaves.

SUMMER

In summer months, you'll see the continuation of the spo-radic flowering of the sweetbay magnolias, and 'March Til Frost', which started in early spring or even late win-ter, will continue to sporadically produce flowers all sum-mer long as will the cultivars of *Magnolia laevifolia*. But the quintessential summer-flowering magnolia is the southern magnolia, *M. grandiflora*, of which there are at least 100 cultivars. All are characterized by having glossy evergreen foliage and large, upward-facing, lemony fra-grant flowers throughout summer. Several cultivars also have a brown "fuzz" or indumentum on the underside of the leaf, which can add to the ornamental characteristic of these plants. This is an iconic southern landscape plant and can be used in a variety of ways. For screening, I like 'D. D. Blanchard', 'Claudia Wannamaker', and 'Bracken's Brown Beauty'. Both Alta 'TMGH' and 'Hasse' are upright selections that are perfect for tight corners. While most *M. grandiflora* cultivars are towering specimens, there are some more diminutive selections for the smaller garden, such as 'Kay Parris', Teddy Bear 'Southern Charm', and Baby Grand 'STRgra'.

Magnolia 'Nimbus' and 'Katie-O Early' are two other interesting summer-flowering cultivars that share *M. virginiana* var. *australis* as a parent. 'Nimbus' has cup-shaped white flowers with a strong lemony fragrance. 'Katie O-Early' has pink, upward-facing, *M. virginiana*–like flowers.

Fragrance

Along with their showy flowers, fragrance is the other attribute that defines many of the ornamental magno-lias. Nearly every magnolia in this book has some fra-grance, ranging from slight or barely detectable to the incredible lemony fragrance of *Magnolia grandiflora* and *M. virginiana* var. *australis*. For anywhere that you might want a magnolia in your landscape, there is undoubtedly a fragrant option that will fit your needs. *Magnolia gran-diflora* 'Kay Parris' is a terrific small tree that will pro-vide lemon-scented flowers throughout summer. It is a great option for smaller gardens. Another favorite is the hybrid *Magnolia* 'Judy Zuk', created at Brooklyn Botanic

Magnolia grandiflora Baby Grand 'STRgra' is a new southern mag-nolia cultivar that holds great promise for small spaces.

Summer-flowering *Magnolia* 'Katie-O Early' is an exciting new evergreen hybrid.

Magnolia foveolata 'Shibamichi' is an evergreen Asian species that smells of canned pears.

Magnolias for Fragrance

Magnolia champaca
Magnolia 'Daybreak'
Magnolia denudata
Magnolia figo and cultivars
Magnolia figo var. *crassipes* 'Purple Queen'
Magnolia ×*foggii* 'Jack Fogg'
Magnolia 'Ginter Spicy White'
Magnolia grandiflora and cultivars
Magnolia 'Heaven Scent'
Magnolia 'Judy Zuk'
Magnolia macrophylla subsp. *ashei*
Magnolia 'Nimbus'
Magnolia 'Porcelain Dove'
Magnolia sieboldii 'Colossus'
Magnolia stellata and cultivars
Magnolia virginiana var. *australis* and cultivars
Magnolia virginiana var. *virginiana*
Magnolia ×*wiesneri* 'Aashild Kalleberg'
Magnolia zenii

A beautiful spring display from *Magnolia cylindrica*, which has a lovely fragrance that comes out in the evening.

Garden and named in honor of their president at the time, which has a fruity fragrance, rare among magnolias. It is very fastigiate with upward-facing, tulip-shaped flowers that are orange-yellow with a blush of pink at the base of the tepals.

Many adjectives have been used to describe the fragrance of magnolia tepals. "Bananalike" is used to describe the smell of *Magnolia figo* 'Port Wine' and *M. figo* var. *crassipes* 'Purple Queen', as well as *M.* ×*foggii* 'Jack Fogg'. Like 'Judy Zuk', *M. insignis* has been described as having a fruitlike fragrance. *Magnolia cylindrica* and *M. delavayi* are fragrant at night. *Magnolia* 'Wim Rutten' has been described as having papayalike fragrance. The tropical *M. champaca* has a strong, spicy fragrance, while *M.* ×*wiesneri* smells of pineapples and *M. foveolata* 'Shibamichi' has been described as smelling like canned pears.

Evergreen Magnolias

Another great attribute of many magnolias is that they are evergreen, and one of the very best for its evergreen attributes is the southern magnolia, *Magnolia grandiflora*, a staple of the winter landscape at Scott Arboretum. Many have considerable hardiness and can be used effectively in Zones 6–7, including cultivars such as 'Bracken's Brown Beauty' and (my favorite) 'D. D. Blanchard'. This large-stature selection grows quickly and has an upright habit; the beautiful shiny leaves face upward and have a luxuriant brown indumentum on their undersides, adding to the tree's ornamental impact.

The sweetbay magnolias (*Magnolia virginiana* var. *australis*) are also excellent for their evergreen leaves. Several cultivars are exceptional, including 'Henry Hicks', 'Satellite', 'Santa Rosa', 'Green Shadow', 'Ned's Northern Belle', 'Mattie Mae Smith', and Sweet Thing 'Perry Paige'. 'Ned's Northern Belle' is an evergreen clone that is good for colder climates. 'Mattie Mae Smith' has yellow and green variegated leaves, and Sweet Thing 'Perry Paige' is a rounded shrub reaching 8 feet (2 m) tall that could be used as a substitute for other broadleaved evergreen shrubs such as rhododendrons, *Kalmia latifolia*, *Ilex glabra*, and cherry laurels. Many of these cultivars also have an attractive silver underside to their leaves, which are revealed when the wind blows.

There are also several relatively new Asian evergreen species that are becoming more available through mail-order nurseries. *Magnolia delavayi* has broad evergreen leaves and sports large, fragrant creamy white flowers in summer. *Magnolia foveolata*, which was the first magnolia we encountered on a collecting trip to the northern mountains of Vietnam in October 2013, is characterized by the golden indumentum on the underside of its leaves. The red lotus tree, *M. insignis*, has been gaining popularity among members of the Magnolia Society International for its upright pyramidal habit and, in particular, its flowers, which can range from creamy white to pink to scarlet. The scarlet flowers are important for breeding purposes, as hybridizers work toward attaining a true red–flowered cultivar. *Magnolia lotungensis* has upward-facing white flowers with distinct purple

Evergreen *Magnolia grandiflora* 'D. D. Blanchard' is a personal favorite for its upright, pyramidal form and attractive brown indumentum on the underside of its leaves.

Magnolia virginiana var. *australis* 'Green Shadow' is one of the most evergreen of the sweetbay magnolias.

Magnolia yuyuanensis is a relatively new evergreen Asian species.

stamens. The monkey forest tree, *M. maudiae*, is a small dense tree with a rounded canopy and an abundance of large white flowers. It is found in the wild in many provinces throughout China. It has been successfully used as a street tree in Portland, Oregon. *Magnolia maudiae* var. *platypetala*, the ivory-flowered michelia, has evergreen leaves, 8 inches (20 cm) long, with a bronze indumentum and a profusion of white, multi-tepaled flowers. Finally, at JC Raulston Arboretum in Raleigh, North Carolina, there is a beautiful specimen of *M. yuyuanensis*. This densely pyramidal tree will reach 30 feet (9 m) tall at maturity. In late spring and throughout summer it is adorned with upward-facing, cup-shaped flowers with red stamens. Of the aforementioned new Asian species, *M. yuyuanensis* has promise as possibly being hardy in Zone 7.

The banana shrub, *Magnolia figo*, and its cultivars 'Port Wine' and *M. figo* var. *crassipes* 'Purple Queen' can be grown successfully in most climates in Zone 7 or above. The small white or purple flowers are borne in early to midspring and have a delicious bananalike fragrance. They can be used for hedging, screening, or as foundation plants.

Evergreens for Small Spaces

Magnolia 'Exotic Star'
Magnolia 'Eternal Spring'
Magnolia Fairy Cream 'MicJur02'
Magnolia figo and cultivars
Magnolia figo var. *crasspipes* 'Purple Queen'
Magnolia ×*foggii* 'Jack Fogg'
Magnolia grandiflora 'Kay Parris'
Magnolia grandiflora Baby Grand 'STRgra'
Magnolia grandiflora Teddy Bear 'Southern Charm'
Magnolia insignis
Magnolia 'Katie-O Early'
Magnolia laevifolia and cultivars
Magnolia 'Twiggy'
Magnolia virginiana var. *australis* Sweet Thing
    'Perry Paige'

Evergreens for Hedges or Screening

Magnolia Fairy Cream 'MicJur02'
Magnolia figo and cultivars
Magnolia figo var. *crassipes* 'Purple Queen'
Magnolia grandiflora and cultivars
Magnolia laevifolia and cultivars
Magnolia 'Twiggy'

Evergreens as Specimen Trees

Magnolia champaca
Magnolia delavayi
Magnolia doltsopa and *M. doltsopa* 'Silver Cloud'
Magnolia foveolata 'Shibamichi'
Magnolia grandiflora and cultivars
Magnolia lotungensis
Magnolia maudiae
Magnolia maudiae var. *platypetala*
Magnolia 'Nimbus'
Magnolia 'Porcelain Dove'
Magnolia virginiana var. *australis* and cultivars
Magnolia yuyuanensis

Magnolia laevifolia 'Michelle' combines evergreen leaves and a profusion of flowers to great effect.

The Fairy Magnolia series is a new group of shrubby magnolias. It includes Fairy Cream, Fairy Blush, and Fairy White. Each has small flowers with a sweet fragrance and can be used in a variety of ways in the landscape where a smaller magnolia is needed.

Magnolia laevifolia can be used as a large shrub or a small tree. Unlike other magnolias, the buds form in the axils of the leaves along the stems, thus producing a more profuse look. The ivory white, chalice-shaped flowers are 4 inches (10 cm) wide and have a boss of striking yellow stamens made up of 6–12 tepals. The buds are covered in a cinnamon indumentum, adding to its ornamental display. A good compact form is 'Strybing Compact'. Flowering can start as early as late winter and continue into autumn depending on your climate. 'Copperstop' has furry stems and leaves with coppery undersides, giving this cultivar its name. 'Michelle' is a profuse-flowering cultivar, 18 feet (5 m) tall and 10 feet (3 m) wide, with good form. 'Snowbird' is more diminutive at 6 feet (2 m) tall and 4 feet (1 m) wide, making it perfect for foundation plantings and hedges. Other *M. laevifolia* cultivars include 'Inspiration' and 'Free Spirit'.

The sweet michelia, *Magnolia doltsopa*, can reach up to 100 feet (30 m) tall, but is more likely to grow to about 35 feet (11 m) in cultivation. Its buds are covered in attractive brown hairs and open to reveal pure white flowers, 5–7 inches (13–18 cm) across, with a heavy fragrance in late winter. The cultivar 'Silver Cloud' is a small, compact tree with a pyramidal or conical habit. It can be used in small gardens and is good for hedging.

Magnolia tripetala has fantastic large leaves that provide a tropical effect in the garden.

Tropical Foliage

While magnolias are predominantly grown for their flowers and fragrance, many possess other attributes that contribute to their overall attraction. There are several species and a handful of cultivars with oversized foliage that can create a tropical effect in the garden. Many of the deciduous North American species have large foliage. The bigleaf magnolia, *Magnolia macrophylla*, has leaves up to 40 inches (102 cm) long and 18 inches (46 cm) wide that are somewhat undulating with attractive silvery white undersides. *Magnolia macrophylla* subsp. *ashei* is essentially a diminutive version of the bigleaf magnolia with leaves up to 24 inches (61 cm) long. The Fraser magnolia, *M. fraseri*, has bold leaves up to 12 inches (30 cm) long. The umbrella magnolia, *M. tripetala*, has very large leaves up to 24 inches (61 cm) long. 'Ginter Spicy White' is a hybrid of *M. tripetala* 'Bloomfield' and *M.* 'R20-1', bred by Bill Smith. Because of the *M. tripetala* parentage, the leaves are large, up to 13 inches (4 m) long. 'Silk Road', with similar parentage (*M. tripetala* × [*M. tripetala* × *M. obovata*]) has attractive large foliage. Houpu magnolia, *M. officinalis*, has elliptic (twice as long as broad) leaves up to 12–16 inches (30–41 cm) long. On the High Line in New York City, several large-leaved native magnolias, including *M. macrophylla*, *M. macrophylla* subsp. *ashei*, and *M. tripetala*, are planted in masses for the provocative effect of their foliage.

The beautiful *Magnolia
stellata* 'Chrysanthe-
mumiflora', with an
abundance of tepals.

Magnolias for Small Spaces

For the small garden or for areas where a small landscape plant is needed there are several magnolias that can fit your needs.

The star magnolia, *Magnolia stellata*, has many cultivars that are relatively small and can be used in smaller landscapes. They bloom in early spring with white or pink flowers, 4 inches (10 cm) across, made up of 12–18 tepals, and are often fragrant. At maturity, they might reach 20 feet (6 m) tall and wide, but there are several that are smaller. 'Chrysanthemumiflora' is 10–15 feet (3–5 m) tall and 10 feet (3 m) wide with soft pink flowers. 'Encore' is similarly sized and has white flowers with a boss of yellow stamens.

The Loebner magnolia, *Magnolia ×loebneri*, is slightly more upright in stature, but has starlike flowers, similar to *M. stellata*. 'Wildcat', 18 feet (5 m) tall and 12 feet (4 m) wide, has soft pink flowers with up to 52 tepals. 'Leonard Messel' is a very popular cultivar with pink flowers in midspring. 'Mag's Pirouette' reaches 12 feet (4 m) tall and has white flowers. 'Donna' has flowers that are pure white and 6–7 inches (15–18 cm) wide—larger and flatter than those of most *M. ×loebneri* cultivars—with 12–13 broad, reflexed tepals. It grows to a diminutive 15 feet (5 m) tall and 12 feet (4 m) wide.

While most of the so-called yellow magnolias can get very large in stature, there are a handful that will stay smaller in the garden, including the hybrids 'Lois', 'Daphne', and 'Golden Gift', along with *M. acuminata* var. *subcordata*.

Magnolias in The Girls series are all excellent small magnolias. While they may eventually broaden to 20 feet (6 m) tall and wide after 50 years, for most of their lives they are well kept and remain relatively compact.

There are also several new introductions that stay small and compact in the landscape. 'Black Tulip' has dark purple flowers and reaches 11 feet (3 m) tall in ten years. From New Zealand, 'Cleopatra', the result of a cross between *Magnolia ×soulangeana* 'Sweet Simplicity' and *M.* 'Black Tulip', has red-purple flowers and reaches 13 feet (4 m) after ten years. 'Genie' is 13 feet (4 m) tall and 6 feet (2 m) wide and sports maroon to magenta flowers. *Magnolia* Fairy Cream 'MicJur02' has a shrubby habit and cream flowers that open from brown velvety buds.

Magnolia acuminata var. *subcordata* is a good choice for a diminutive, yellow native for the garden.

Magnolias for Small Spaces

The Girls series
Magnolia 'Genie'
Magnolia 'Golden Gift'
Magnolia grandiflora Baby Grand 'STRgra'
Magnolia grandiflora Teddy Bear 'Southern
    Charm'
Magnolia grandiflora 'Kay Parris'
Magnolia macrophylla subsp. *ashei*
Magnolia ×*soulangeana* 'Lilliputian'

Magnolia ×*soulangeana* cultivars 'Lennei' and 'Lilliputian' are terrific spring-flowering options for small spaces.

The flowers, 2.5 inches (6 cm) across, are borne along the stem, providing a magnificent floral show. It sporadically reblooms in summer and autumn. *Magnolia* Honey Tulip 'JURmag5' has goblet-shaped early yellow flowers and reaches 13 feet (4 m) tall and 12 feet (4 m) wide.

Magnolia laevifolia can be used as either a small tree or a large shrub. 'Strybing Compact' and 'Snowbird' are two of the more compact selections.

The saucer magnolia, *Magnolia* ×*soulangeana*, is generally large in stature, but there are a couple that are more appropriate for the small garden. 'Lennei' reaches 15–20 feet (5–6 m) tall and wide and has a bicolored flower of white on the interior and pink on the exterior of the tepals. 'Lilliputian' only reaches 12 feet (4 m) tall and 8 feet (2 m) wide and has a tight pyramidal habit. It produces an abundance of fragrant pink flowers.

Of the large-leaved native magnolias, the Ashe magnolia, *Magnolia macrophylla* subsp. *ashei*, is the best for its small stature. Reaching only 20 feet (6 m) tall at maturity, this small tree still displays all the attributes of *M. macrophylla* with large leaves and large white, open-faced, fragrant flowers with a purple central splotch. On my small property in Swarthmore, since I only have room for a few magnolias, the Ashe magnolia grows in my woodland garden and shows off its bold foliage.

Magnolia 'Twiggy' is a densely compact pyramidal tree reaching 16 feet (5 m) tall and 12 feet (4 m) wide after 13 years.

Magnolia 'Judy Zuk' at Scott Arboretum. This beautiful cultivar has it all: it is late flowering, upright, good for tight spaces, and has a fruity fragrance and a suffusion of pink and yellow flowers.

Fastigiate Magnolias

Sometimes you might find yourself wanting to fit a tall tree into a tight space. Fastigiate magnolias, which are generally compact and upward pointing, are perfect for such situations. In the Garden of Fragrance at Swarthmore College, we had a very tight corner where we wanted to use a plant that could grow fairly tall without getting too wide and encroaching on the adjacent pathway. Eventually we settled on the very fastigiated *Magnolia grandiflora* 'Hasse', which after almost 30 years turned out to be a perfect choice. *Magnolia grandiflora* Alta 'TMGH' is another good choice to fit this need.

Magnolia 'Sun Spire' is a very fastigiate yellow magnolia reaching 15–20 feet (5–6 m) tall and 6 feet (2 m) wide. The deep yellow flowers range from soft to medium yellow. *Magnolia* 'Judy Zuk', a complex hybrid, also remains very upright and only slightly broadens over time. Most of the yellow magnolias, however, are much more broad spreading.

Another fastigiate tree, *Magnolia* 'Daybreak', is considered to be among the best of all magnolias. August Kehr, the hybridizer, considers this one of his finest introductions. The rose-pink flowers are borne in midspring and are extremely fragrant. At maturity it is very columnar in

Magnolias for Tight Spaces

Magnolia 'Caerhays Belle'
Magnolia 'Cleopatra'
Magnolia 'Daybreak'
Magnolia denudata 'Swarthmore Sentinel'
Magnolia grandiflora Alta 'TMGH'
Magnolia grandiflora 'Hasse'
Magnolia 'Judy Zuk'
Magnolia 'Rose Marie'
Magnolia 'Silk Road'
Magnolia 'Sun Spire'
Magnolia 'Yellow Lantern'

Many in the Magnolia Society International consider 'Daybreak' to be in the top five of all magnolias.

shape, 40 feet (12 m) tall and 15 feet (5 m) wide. This is also one of the hardiest of the magnolias.

For early spring flowers, look to the fastigiate *Magnolia denudata* 'Swarthmore Sentinel', a fast-growing tree with a spirelike habit. The fragrant flowers are pure white.

Topiary and Espaliers

Many magnolias, especially many of the evergreen types, lend themselves to being manipulated into hedges and topiary, and can be used for espaliering. Hand pruning tends to work best. Using manual or electric hedge shears will end up cutting too many leaves in half, leaving them unsightly. *Magnolia grandiflora* is probably the best subject for pruning into a topiary or an espalier. At Bartlett Tree Research Laboratories and Arboretum in Charlotte,

Magnolias for Espaliers

Magnolia grandiflora
Magnolia grandiflora Alta 'TMGH'
Magnolia grandiflora Baby Grand 'STRgra'
Magnolia grandiflora 'Bracken's Brown Beauty'
Magnolia grandiflora 'Claudia Wannamaker'
Magnolia grandiflora 'D. D. Blanchard'
Magnolia grandiflora 'Hasse'
Magnolia grandiflora 'Kay Parris'
Magnolia laevifolia
Magnolia laevifolia 'Copperstop'
Magnolia laevifolia 'Michelle'
Magnolia laevifolia 'Snowbird'

Magnolia grandiflora 'Kay Parris' espaliered at Bartlett Tree Research Laboratories and Arboretum in Charlotte, North Carolina.

Magnolias for Screening

Magnolia doltsopa 'Silver Cloud'
Magnolia Fairy Cream 'MicJur02'
Magnolia figo 'Port Wine'
Magnolia figo var. *crassipes* 'Purple Queen'
Magnolia grandiflora and cultivars
Magnolia insignis 'Anita Figlar'
Magnolia laevifolia and cultivars
Magnolia maudiae
Magnolia virginiana var. *australis* and cultivars

A great example of the *Magnolia grandiflora* cultivar 'Claudia Wannamaker' used for screening.

North Carolina, there is a wonderful specimen of *M. grandiflora* 'Kay Parris' espaliered into horizontal tiers. At Miliken Arboretum in Spartanburg, South Carolina, a long row of 'Claudia Wannamaker' has been hand trimmed into a tight hedge. Several years ago I was on a tour of the gardens of Lake District in northern Italy (Lake Como and Lake Maggiore). At our hotel there was a large two-story *M. grandiflora* that was being hand pruned by a gardener on scaffolding. It was pruned into a perfect gum-drop shape. *Magnolia laevifolia*, *M. figo*, and *M.* 'Twiggy' also lend themselves to this type of pruning.

Magnolias with Attractive Fruit

While their flowers get most of the attention, many magnolias also sport beautiful fruit. The fruit of a magnolia is an aggregate of follicles (dry cavities, each one with a seed), a conelike structure that can be fairly prominent. The cone can turn from pink to red in

A display of fruit from *Magnolia sieboldii*.

Magnolias with Attractive Fruit

Magnolia grandiflora
Magnolia grandiflora Alta 'TMGH'
Magnolia grandiflora 'Bracken's Brown Beauty'
Magnolia grandiflora 'Claudia Wannamaker'
Magnolia grandiflora 'D. D. Blanchard'
Magnolia macrophylla subsp. *ashei*
Magnolia officinalis
Magnolia sieboldii
Magnolia tripetala
Magnolia virginiana var. *australis*

autumn. Once the follicles open they can reveal an individual shiny red seed that also is attractive. In particular, almost all selections of *Magnolia grandiflora* have attractive fruit, up to 5 inches (13 cm) long, which will turn to pink. The structure will eventually split open revealing orange-red seed that dangles on a tiny threadlike appendage. The fruit ripens from early to late autumn and is attractive to wildlife. *Magnolia macrophylla* and *M. macrophylla* subsp. *ashei* also have attractive fruit, 2–4 inches (5–10 cm) long, that is very pubescent (hairy) and can turn from pink to reddish-orange at maturity. *Magnolia virginiana* var. *australis* and *M. virginiana* var. *virginiana* have clusters of attractive shiny red fruit in late summer or early autumn. *Magnolia wilsonii* and *M. sieboldii* have small pink, ornamental fruit, 1–3 inches (3–8 cm) long. *Magnolia officinalis* has large fruit, up to 5 inches (13 cm) long, that turn red with bright red seeds.

Flower Color

While magnolias are generally recognized for their soft pink or pure white flowers, other flower colors are easy to come by. Almost every shade of pink and purple exist, from pale pink to nearly white, bubblegum pink and deep pinks to nearly magenta. Light purple flowers can be found, as well—flowers that are known as red, but are

The beautiful white flowers of *Magnolia salicifolia* come early.

The small, evergreen *Magnolia laevifolia* 'Michelle' has a great abundance of white flowers.

closer to a reddish purple or wine-red. White dominates many of the straight species, but the color is also prevalent among cultivars. Yellow was the most coveted color for years, and a number of hybrids can be found with various shades of yellow flowers. *Magnolia champaca* is nearly orange, and the relatively new *Magnolia insignis* produces nearly red flowers.

WHITE

Many ornamental magnolias have white flowers. A large specimen of *Magnolia denudata*, *M. kobus*, or *M. salicifolia* can look stunning in the landscape. Many of the white-flowering deciduous cultivars, such as 'Anticipation', 'David Clulow', 'Ivory Chalice', or 'Milky Way', might benefit from being juxtaposed against an evergreen backdrop of, say, *Cryptomeria japonica*, *Thuja* 'Green Giant', *Picea orientalis*, *Ilex aquifolium*, *I. opaca*, or *I. ×altaclerensis*, among others. Some of the smaller white-flowering magnolias, such as *Magnolia stellata* and *M. ×loebneri*, can often have a powerful impact in the landscape planted in groups of three and five. Several of the evergreen magnolias have white flowers, including *M. grandiflora*, *M. virginiana* var. *australis*, *M. yuyuanensis*, *M. lotungensis*, *M.*

laevifolia, and *M. doltsopa*. Their own foliage provides a nice contrast to the flowers and helps make the plants more visible in the landscape.

YELLOW

Yellow-flowering magnolias, introduced by Brooklyn Botanic Garden, were a huge breakthrough in magnolia breeding in the 1970s. For years the yellow magnolia was considered the Holy Grail of the genus. *Magnolia* 'Elizabeth', named in 1978, has clear, upward-facing primrose yellow flowers from long, tapering buds with 6–9 tepals. The flowers, 8 inches (20 cm) across, open up as they mature to reveal red stamens. While this cultivar is a soft yellow, it was the first of many more hybrids and cultivars and subsequent releases that had brighter yellow, golden yellow, and orange-yellow flowers. Today, there are more than 60 cultivars of yellow magnolias. This book features many of the best, including some with a small stature like 'Daphne', Honey Tulip 'JURmag5', 'Lois', and 'Golden Gift'. Others produce abundant flowers, such as 'Butterflies', 'Yellow Bird', and 'Sunsation'. Those with light or soft yellow flowers would benefit from the backdrop of an evergreen tree to help make the color pop. *Magnolia champaca* and *M*. 'Judy Zuk' have orange-yellow flowers.

Magnolia 'Butterflies' is one of the very best of the early-flowering yellow magnolias.

Magnolia 'Yellow Bird' has beautiful yellow tulip- or chalice-shaped flowers.

A beautiful specimen of the pink-flowering *Magnolia* 'Galaxy' at Scott Arboretum.

PINK

Pink is a color that dominates the magnolia world, even if the category can include anything from salmon to cerise to magenta to bubblegum, and so on. All the species and cultivars that have pink flowers are striking enough on their own that an evergreen backdrop is not necessary to help show them off. However, pink-, white-, and purple-flowering magnolias all combine nicely and harmoniously in the landscape.

Nearly all saucer magnolia cultivars are pink. Cultivars of both *Magnolia stellata* and *M. ×loebneri* have great pink flowers, including *M. stellata* 'Chrysanthemumiflora' and 'Royal Star' and *M. ×loebneri* 'Leonard Messel' and 'Wildcat'. The Girls, including 'Ann', 'Betty', 'Jane', and 'Susan', have varying shades of pink flowers. *Magnolia sprengeri* var. *diva* 'Diva' is an exquisitely beautiful specimen tree. Many pink-flowering cultivars represent several of the very best magnolias, including 'Coral Lake', 'Daybreak', 'Galaxy', 'Spectrum', 'Star Wars', and *M. sargentiana* var. *robusta*.

Pink-Flowering Magnolias

Magnolia 'Caerhays Belle'
Magnolia 'Coral Lake'
Magnolia 'Betty'
Magnolia dawsoniana
Magnolia 'Daybreak'
Magnolia 'Galaxy'
Magnolia sargentiana var. *robusta*
Magnolia sprengeri var. *diva* 'Diva'
Magnolia 'Star Wars'
Magnolia stellata 'Chrysanthemumiflora'
Magnolia ×loebneri 'Leonard Messel'
Magnolia ×soulangeana 'Alexandrina'

Magnolia 'Spectrum', a sister seedling of 'Galaxy', seen here growing at Scott Arboretum.

Purple-Flowering Magnolias

Magnolia 'Black Tulip'
Magnolia campbellii 'Darjeeling'
Magnolia figo 'Port Wine'
Magnolia figo var. *crassipes* 'Purple Queen'
Magnolia 'Purple Prince'

PURPLE

The true purple-flowering magnolias are represented by only a handful of cultivars. Many that might be described as purple are actually pinkish purple. 'Black Tulip' has goblet-shaped flowers, 6 inches (15 cm) across, that are red-wine in color. *Magnolia figo* cultivars have purple notes. 'Port Wine' has purple-tinged flowers and can bloom for up to four to six weeks. *Magnolia figo* var. *crassipes* 'Purple Queen' has deep red-purple flowers edged in white. 'Purple Prince' is a hybrid between *M. liliiflora* 'Darkest Purple' and *M.* ×*soulangeana* 'Lennei'. The long, slender buds open into a cup-and-saucer-shaped flower, 10 inches (25 cm) across, with 9 tepals that are 5 inches (13 cm) long and dark purple and slightly lighter on inner tepal.

RED

The *new* Holy Grail of the magnolia world is one that has flowers that are true red. Like other colors, red is often interpreted as reddish pink or reddish purple, but now with the emergence of red-flowered forms of *Magnolia insignis*, true red-flowering magnolias are becoming a reality. Felix 'JURmag2' has large open-faced, water lily–like flowers, 12 inches (30 cm) across, with deep rose-red color resulting from a cross of *M.* 'Atlas' and *M.* 'Vulcan'. The August Kehr introduction, 'March Til Frost', has upright, goblet-shaped flowers, 5–8 inches (13–20 cm) across, with deep wine-red outer tepals and rose-white inner tepals, making for a striking contrast. Dennis Ledvina's 'Red Baron' has large goblet-shaped flowers that are deep rose-red with a white interior. *Magnolia insignis* 'Anita Figlar' is more profuse than straight *M. insignis*. The flowers have 9 tepals in 3 tiers of 3 tepals each with the outer 3

The evergreen and shrublike *Magnolia figo* var. *crasspipes* 'Purple Queen' has striking clusters of purple flowers.

Red-Flowering Magnolias

Magnolia 'Black Tulip'
Magnolia Felix 'JURmag2'
Magnolia 'Genie'
Magnolia 'March Til Frost'
Magnolia 'Vulcan'
Magnolia campbellii 'Darjeeling'
Magnolia 'Cleopatra'
Magnolia 'Frank's Masterpiece'
Magnolia insignis
Magnolia insignis 'Anita Figlar'
Magnolia 'Red Baron'

tepals reflexing downward. The inner tier is a deep red on both sides of the tepal and the smaller inner tepal is pale pink to white. This creates a bicolored effect up close, but from afar the flowers look red. The flowers last for two to three days. This cultivar has become an important breeding parent with many new hybrids.

Companion Plants

Many magnolias have very dense surface roots, making them more difficult to garden under. However, in general, dry shade–loving perennials will thrive in these conditions: examples include *Epimedium, Asarum, Polystichum, Dryopteris* and many sedges, *Carex*. For some of the evergreen magnolias, especially *Magnolia grandiflora*, growing almost any plant underneath will be extremely difficult. The combination of the roots and the thick evergreen foliage prohibits most moisture from getting to the ground beneath.

Magnolia insignis 'Anita Figlar', a new evergreen introduction, has nearly red flowers.

UNDERSTANDING MAGNOLIAS

T

The genus *Magnolia* is fairly wide ranging, from evergreens to deciduous trees and shrubs. The leaves are alternate and can range from the relatively small, like the evergreen leaves of *M. laevifolia*, to the very large, like those of the bigleaf magnolia, *M. macrophylla*. The leaves can be fairly coarse and leathery, like those of *M. grandiflora*, and can also have an attractive indumentum on the underside of the leaf, as is the case with *M. grandiflora* (brown) and *M. foveolata* (golden). In short, there's more variety among the genus than it would first appear.

Magnolia flowers are borne solitary and composed of 6 or more petallike tepals. Unlike other flowering plants where the petals and sepals are clearly differentiated, this is not the case with magnolias (the term *tepals* was created for just this scenario). Tepals, which make up the showy part of magnolia flowers, may occur in two whorls, an inner and an outer, and may differ in number, size, and color. They mostly occur terminally, but in some species they occur on axillary shoots. In the center of each flower is an elongated receptacle with several spirally arranged stamens. The stamens can be creamy white or an attractive golden yellow, red, or purple.

The fruit is an aggregate of follicles. Each follicle produces one or more seeds, and the seeds often have attractive shiny red seed coats. The aggregate of follicles can look like a little cucumber—see for example the appropriately named cucumber tree, *Magnolia acuminata*—or can be fairly large and barrel shaped like the fruits of *M. grandiflora* and *M. officinalis*. The color of the fruit might start out green or creamy green but can turn to pink, pinkish red, and sometimes red and be an attractive ornamental attribute. After the seed dehisce (split open at maturity), the follicle can turn brown and become woody; it will often persist on the plant for some time.

Magnolia foveolata 'Shibamichi' is a beautiful and unusual evergreen magnolia with golden indumentum.

The voluptuous white flowers of *Magnolia* 'Sayonara', bred by Todd Gresham, have a blush of pink at the base of the tepals.

A closeup of the purplish pink flowers of *Magnolia* 'Galaxy', a William Kosar hybrid from 1963.

Taxonomy

Magnolia is a member of the family Magnoliaceae, and since 2000, major taxonomic changes have occurred in the genus. Studies of DNA have led to many previous genera such as *Michelia* and *Manglietia* being included in the genus. Today, only two genera are recognized as members of the Magnoliaceae, *Magnolia* and *Liriodendron*, the tulip tree, where there are two species, *L. tulipifera* and *L. chinense*. The genus *Magnolia* is divided into multiple sections including *Michelia* (*M. foveolata*, *M. figo*, *M. champaca*); *Yulania* (*M. kobus*, *M. stellata*, *M. salicifolia*, *M. denudata*, *M. dawsoniana*); *Gynopodium*;

Manglietiastrum; *Kmeria*; *Magnolia* (*M. virginiana*, *M. grandiflora*); *Manglietia* (*M. insignis*); *Rhytidospermum* (*M. sieboldii*, *M. wilsonii*, *M. tripetala*, *M. officinalis*); *Macrophylla* (*M. macrophylla*, *M. macrophylla* subsp. *ashei*); *Auriculata* (*M. fraseri*); *Gwillimia* (*M. delavayi*); and *Talauma*. Section *Yulania* represents the most species with ornamental attributes and many have been extensively used in breeding work.

Hybridization

Magnolia hybridization has been popular as long as magnolias have been cultivated as ornamental plants. Hybridizers create crosses (hybrids) in order to improve on flower color, fragrance, and size (smaller magnolias are particularly sought after). The practice dates back to 1820 when Étienne Soulange-Bodin hybridized *M. denudata* with *M. liliiflora* to create the now world-famous saucer magnolia, *M. ×soulangeana*. Todd Gresham, a founding member of the Magnolia Society from Santa Cruz, California, then made hundreds of crosses resulting in many popular cultivars such as 'Tina Durio', 'Sayonara', and 'Royal Crown'.

In 1960, Phil Savage began breeding magnolias in Bloomfield Hills, Michigan. He focused on later-flowering hybrids, often using *Magnolia denudata* as a parent. Some of his most noteworthy hybrids include 'Big Dude', 'Butterflies', and 'Yellow Lantern'. In 1955, Francis deVos at US National Arboretum began a hybridization program using *M. liliiflora* 'Nigra' and *M. stellata* 'Rosea'. This resulted in the very famous The Girls series, made up of eight hybrids, including 'Ann', 'Jane', 'Susan', and 'Betty', among others. Also at the National Arboretum in 1963, William Kosar hybridized *M. liliiflora* 'Nigra' with *M. sprengeri* var. *diva* 'Diva' to produce 'Galaxy' and 'Spectrum', two magnolias that are still popular today.

Brooklyn Botanic Garden hybridizers Eva Maria Serber, Doris Stone, and Lola Koerting were instrumental in the creation of the so-called yellow magnolias, including the much-loved 'Elizabeth'. August Kehr from Hendersonville, North Carolina, followed up on their work by introducing his *Magnolia acuminata* × *M. denudata* hybrids, including 'Sundance' and 'Daybreak', among others. New Zealander Felix Jury was also a prolific hybridizer. 'Mark Jury', named for his son, is a suspected hybrid between *M. campbellii* subsp. *mollicomata* 'Lanarth' and *M. sargentiana* var. *robusta*. It is a breeding parent of other important Jury hybrids, including 'Atlas', 'Iolanthe', 'Athene', and 'Vulcan'. Mark Jury has carried on the Jury legacy and continues to hybridize magnolias today. Some of his introductions include 'Black Tulip', Burgundy Star 'JURmag4', and his newest release, Honey Tulip 'JURmag5'.

Other modern-day magnolia breeders of significance include fellow kiwi Vance Hooper, who runs the Magnolia Grove garden in Taranaki. His introductions include a complex hybrid named 'Brixton Belle' (a cross between 'Sweet Simplicity' × 'Black Tulip' and 'Sir Harold Hillier'), as well as 'Cameo', 'Cleopatra', and the exquisite 'Genie'.

Today, hybridizers such as Bill Smith from Virginia and the late Dennis Ledvina in Wisconsin are making remarkable breakthroughs with magnolia hybridization. Ledvina used a variety of breeding parents to create a myriad of traits, such as large skyward-facing

A beautiful, large specimen of *Magnolia* 'Spectrum', another William Kosar hybrid, at Scott Arboretum.

flowers and striking purple stamens from the parentage of *Magnolia sieboldii*. Some of his most stunning cultivars include 'Exotic Star', 'Oriental Charm', and 'Angel Mist'. Other hybridizers are working on a multitude of attributes, including red- and pink-flowered evergreen magnolias using the pinkish red–flowering *M. insignis* 'Anita Figlar' and hybridizing with other species to introduce hardiness.

Where Magnolias Grow in the Wild

The genus and family have great interest from an evolutionary perspective, as well. Floral parts are arranged in spirals whereas with most other flowering plants the arrangement is in rings. In the late Cretaceous and Tertiary periods, Magnoliaceae was found throughout the Northern Hemisphere. Fossils of magnolias have been discovered in Idaho, eastern Washington, and near Los Angeles. Today, the geographical distribution is disjunct, with two-thirds occurring in Asia and the remaining species found in North America, Central America, northern South America, and scattered through the Caribbean Islands.

Since 2005, there have been 225 recognized species of magnolias in the wild. Magnolias can be found in Ontario, Canada (*Magnolia acuminata*), and there are several species mainly east of the Mississippi River (*M. acuminata*, *M. fraseri*, *M. grandiflora*, *M. virginiana* var. *australis*, *M. virginiana* var. *virginiana*, *M. macrophylla*, *M. macrophylla* subsp. *ashei*, and *M. tripetala*). In Cuba, there are 7 species, including a disjunct population of *M. virginiana* var. *australis*. In Mexico, there are over 24 species with more still being identified. Through Central America, magnolias are found in native habitats in Belize, Costa Rica, Guatemala, El Salvador, Honduras, and Panama. The Caribbean, too, has native magnolias in Martinique, Trinidad, Guadeloupe, St. Vincent, Dominica, Dominican Republic, Haiti, and Puerto Rico, among others. In South America, there are over 30 species in Colombia, but other species are found in Ecuador, Venezuela, Peru, Brazil, and Bolivia.

In Asia, magnolias are found in China with more species there than in any other country, though plants can still be found in the wild in Japan, Korea, Vietnam, India, Sri Lanka, Myanmar, Laos, Cambodia, Thailand, Taiwan, Nepal, Bhutan, Malaysia, Indonesia, Philippines, Singapore, and Papua New Guinea.

There are threats to all of this, of course. In many regions of the world, magnolias are both rare and endangered by development, timber harvesting, and so on, a phenomenon certainly not specific to this genus. The International Union for the Conservation of Nature recognizes a number of magnolia plants that are threatened in their native habitats. Their Red List includes 31 species of magnolias as critically endangered, 58 endangered, 23 vulnerable, and 9 near threatened. Many conservation organizations such as Magnolia Society International, Botanical Gardens Conservation International, and Global Trees Campaign work to conserve the biodiversity of magnolias in the wild.

Magnolia 'Ann'

'Ann' is one of a group of eight magnolias, known as The Girls, selected by the US National Arboretum in 1962. The specimen at Scott Arboretum was received in the same year and has grown 15 feet (5 m) tall with a spread of 22 feet (7 m) over 52 years. This particular cultivar flowers in early spring in Zone 8b, earlier than others in the series. For many years, 'Ann' will remain a relatively small magnolia, making it great for courtyard gardens.

SIZE AND HABIT After 50 years, 15 feet tall (5 m), 22 feet (7 m) wide. Broadly rounded small tree or large shrub.

ZONES 4–7

FLOWERS Reddish purple on the outside and fading to clear pink within; 2–4 inches (5–10 cm) across, with 6–8 tepals. Blooms midspring.

FOLIAGE Elliptic.

CULTIVATION Full sun with well-drained soil. Propagate by cuttings or grafting.

ORIGIN *Magnolia liliiflora* 'Nigra' × *M. stellata* 'Rosea', bred by Francis deVos.

Magnolia 'Anticipation'

This hybrid was the result of seed that was distributed by the Magnolia Society International seed exchange, where it was listed as *Magnolia cylindrica*. It was then grown on by August Kehr. It has a good upright form. Blooms late winter in Tallahassee, Florida (Zone 8b).

SIZE AND HABIT 16–26 feet (5–8 m) tall, 10–12 feet (3–4 m) wide. Upright.
ZONES 6–8
FLOWERS White; 10–12 inches (25–30 cm) across. Blooms early spring.
FOLIAGE Obovate.
CULTIVATION Full sun with well-drained soil. Propagate by cuttings or grafting.
ORIGIN Most likely a hybrid of *M. cylindrica*, bred by August Kehr.

Magnolia 'Athene'

A sister to 'Lotus' and 'Milky Way', 'Athene' was an Award of Garden Merit winner in 2012. We have tried one of these at Swarthmore; they are hardy, but would benefit from some protection from the cold. They bloom in early spring in Tallahassee, Florida (Zone 8b).

SIZE AND HABIT 18–25 feet (5–8 m) tall and wide. Upright when young; rounded at maturity.
ZONES 7–9
FLOWERS Soft pink to white with deeper pink at base of tepals. Open, goblet-shaped flowers, 8–10 inches (20–25 cm) across, sometimes up to 14 inches (36 cm), with 8 tepals. Blooms early spring. Fragrant.
FOLIAGE Elliptic.
CULTIVATION Full sun with well-drained soil. Propagate by cuttings or grafting.
ORIGIN *Magnolia* ×*soulangeana* 'Lennei Alba' × *M.* 'Mark Jury', bred by Felix Jury.

Magnolia 'Betty'

Another of The Girls hybrids produced by the National Arboretum in the early 1960s, 'Betty' flowers later than 'Ann'. Its habit is more tree-like in the United States, while in the British Isles it tends to be shrubbier. New growth has a copper color. Much like 'Ann', 'Betty' is a great magnolia for the small garden.

SIZE AND HABIT After 50 years, 15 feet (5 m) tall, 26 feet (8 m) wide. Broadly rounded small tree or large shrub.
ZONES 4–7
FLOWERS White on inside surface of tepals, with light purple at the base of the outside surface, moving to red-purple at the apex; 8–10 inches (20–25 cm) across, with 12–19 tepals. Blooms midspring.
FOLIAGE Obovate (oval shaped with narrower end at base).
CULTIVATION Full sun with well-drained soil. Propagate by cuttings or grafting.
ORIGIN *Magnolia liliiflora* 'Nigra' × *M. stellata* 'Rosea', bred by William Kosar.

Magnolia biondii

Chinese willow-leaf magnolia

Chinese willow-leaf magnolia is something of a collector's tree and more suitable to the West Coast and Southeast United States, southern England, and other similar climates, where it is warm enough in late winter and early spring for the flowers to not be killed by the cold.

SIZE AND HABIT 30 feet (9 m) tall, 15 feet (5 m) wide. Medium-sized tree with a single or multiple stems.
ZONES 6a–9b
FLOWERS White with pink to purple splotches at base of outer tepals; relatively small and 4 inches (10 cm) across when fully open, with 9–12 tepals. Blooms late winter. Slight fragrance.
FOLIAGE Elliptic.
FRUIT Cylindrical; bright red in autumn.
CULTIVATION Full sun with moisture-retentive soil. Propagate by seed or cuttings.
ORIGIN Native to Gansu, Henan, Hubei, Hunan, Shaanxi, and Sichuan, China.

Magnolia 'Black Tulip'

One of the darkest of the black-purple–flowering magnolias. With cool temperatures and ample moisture, it can experience some rebloom in mid-summer. It blooms the first week of March in Raleigh, North Carolina (Zone 7b).

SIZE AND HABIT After ten years, 11 feet (3 m) tall, 5 feet (2 m) wide. Small, upright tree.
ZONES 5–8
FLOWERS Red-wine and goblet shaped; 6 inches (15 cm) across. Blooms early spring. Fragrant.
FOLIAGE Ovate.
CULTIVATION Full sun with well-drained soil. Propagate by cuttings or grafting.
ORIGIN *Magnolia* 'Vulcan' × *M.* 'Iolanthe', bred by Mark Jury.

Magnolia 'Blushing Belle'

Similar to 'Caerhays Belle', but much hardier. Even at temperatures as low as −20°F (−29°C), there will be no bud damage.

SIZE AND HABIT 15–20 feet (5–6 m) tall, 8–10 feet (2–3 m) wide. Upright.
ZONES 4–9
FLOWERS Deep pink exterior and lighter pink interior; open faced. Blooms early spring. Very pleasant fragrance.
FOLIAGE Obovate.
CULTIVATION Full sun with well-drained soil. Propagate by cuttings or grafting.
ORIGIN *Magnolia* 'Yellow Bird' × *M.* 'Caerhays Belle', bred by Dennis Ledvina.

Magnolia ×*brooklynensis* 'Eva Maria'

Named for Eva Maria Sperber, a hybridizer at Brooklyn Botanic Garden.

SIZE AND HABIT 25 feet (8 m) tall, 17 feet (5 m) wide. Large shrub or small tree.
ZONES 5–9
FLOWERS Tulip shaped with a suffusion of rose, yellow, and green. The 6 tepals are 4 inches (10 cm) long. Blooms midspring.
FOLIAGE Ovate, with silver undersides.
CULTIVATION Full sun with well-drained soil. Propagate by cuttings or grafting.
ORIGIN *Magnolia acuminata* × *M. liliiflora* 'Nigra', bred by Eva Maria Sperber and Doris Stone, Brooklyn Botanic Garden.

Magnolia ×brooklynensis 'Hattie Carthan'

A great, small flowering tree. It blooms one to two weeks later than *Magnolia ×soulangeana* and therefore rarely runs the risk of getting frosted.

SIZE AND HABIT 20 feet (6 m) tall, 15 feet (5 m) wide. Pyramidally shaped large shrub or small tree.
ZONES 5
FLOWERS Yellow and goblet shaped; tepals are 4–5 inches (10–13 cm) long, with slight streaks of purplish pink. Outer whorls of tepals have a green tinge as the foliage emerges. Blooms midspring, sometimes repeat flowering into summer. Fragrant.
FOLIAGE Broadly elliptic.
CULTIVATION Full sun with well-drained soil. Propagate by cuttings or grafting.
ORIGIN *Magnolia ×brooklynensis* 'Eva Maria' × *M. ×brooklynensis* BBGRC #209, bred by Doris Stone.

Magnolia ×brooklynensis 'Woodsman'

The flowers of this yellow magnolia are large and darker than those of 'Eva Maria', which has similar parentage.

SIZE AND HABIT 30 feet (9 m) tall, 20 feet (6 m) wide. Conical when young, becoming more broad spreading over time.
ZONES 4–9
FLOWERS The yellow, green, purple, and rose tepals are borne on upright flowers. Flowering occurs late spring, usually after the chance of frost has passed.
FOLIAGE Broadly elliptic.
CULTIVATION Full sun with well-drained soil. Propagate by cuttings or grafting.
ORIGIN *Magnolia acuminata* 'Klassen' × *M. liliiflora* 'O'Neil', bred by J. C. McDaniel.

Magnolia 'Butterflies'

One of the earliest-flowering yellow magnolias—blooms emerge before foliage—and considered by many to be one of the finest. At Scott Arboretum, it has been our favorite, with a profusion of yellow flowers in late April. It thrives in both the cold and the heat.

SIZE AND HABIT 25–30 feet (8–9 m) tall, 10–15 feet (3–5 m) wide. Upright, pyramidal.

ZONES 4b–9

FLOWERS Deep canary yellow and upward facing; and 3–5 inches (8–13 cm) across, with red stamens and 10–16 tepals. Blooms midspring. Slight lemon fragrance.

FOLIAGE Oblong-elliptic.

CULTIVATION Full sun with well-drained soil. Propagate by cuttings or grafting.

ORIGIN *Magnolia acuminata* 'Fertile Myrtle' × *M. denudata* 'Sawada's Cream', bred by Phil Savage.

Magnolia 'Caerhays Belle'

Blooms in early spring in temperate climates. Because it blooms early, it runs the risk of getting frosted. Hybridized and named at Caerhays Castle in Cornwall, England. An Award of Garden Merit winner in 2012.

SIZE AND HABIT 40 feet (12 m) tall, 25 feet (8 m) wide. Upright to fastigiate to pyramidal.
ZONES 6a–9
FLOWERS Salmon-pink with striking red stamens; 12 inches (30 cm) across, with 12 spoon-shaped tepals, giving them more architecture than on many magnolias. Blooms late winter. Fragrant.
FOLIAGE Obovate.
FRUIT Attractive pink follicles.
CULTIVATION Full sun with well-drained soil. Propagate by cuttings or grafting.
ORIGIN *Magnolia sargentiana* var. *robusta* × *M. sprengeri* var. *diva* 'Diva', bred by Charles Michael.

Magnolia 'Caerhays Surprise'

The *Magnolia liliiflora* parentage brings heat tolerance to this *M. campbellii*–like magnolia. An Award of Garden Merit winner in 2012.

SIZE AND HABIT 15 feet (5 m) tall, 12 feet (4 m) wide. Small tree.
ZONES 5a–8b
FLOWERS Pinkish lavender on inner tepals and deep reddish purple on the outsides; 8–10 inches (20–25 cm) across, with 9–12 tepals; outer tepals are reflexed. Flowers are borne on the ends of arching shoots, giving the flowers a nodding appearance. Blooms early spring.
FOLIAGE Obovate.
CULTIVATION Full sun with well-drained soil. Propagate by cuttings or grafting.
ORIGIN *Magnolia campbellii* subsp. *mollicomata* × *M. liliiflora* 'Nigra', bred by Philip Tregunna.

Magnolia campbellii

Campbell's magnolia

A most magnificent magnolia that is coveted by gardeners around the world, but can only be successfully cultivated in areas like San Francisco to British Columbia, Canada, and England (Zones 8–10). White-flowering forms have been found in the wild, and these have now been introduced into cultivation. Flowers are susceptible to early frosts. Blooms in late winter to early spring in England. There are many excellent cultivars, such as the late-flowering 'Betty Jessel', with crimson flowers; 'Darjeeling', with dark pink flowers; and *Magnolia campbellii* var. *alba* 'Strybing White', for its drooping white tepals.

SIZE AND HABIT Over 70 feet (21 m) tall in cultivation in southern England and over 100 feet (30 m) tall in the wild; 50 feet (15 m) wide. Broadly pyramidal, often multi-stemmed.
ZONES 7–9
FLOWERS Clear pink or white and bowl shaped; 10 inches (25 cm) across, with 12–16 tepals. Inner tepals are erect and outer tepals are flat. Blooms late winter. Fragrant.
FOLIAGE Elliptic.
FRUIT Long, erect, attractive pinkish-red fruits.
CULTIVATION Sheltered but sunny location. Propagate by seed, cuttings, or grafting.
ORIGIN Native to the Himalayas from eastern Nepal to western Yunnan. Found between 7,000–11,000 feet (2,134–3,353 m) in elevation in the wild.

Magnolia campbellii 'Darjeeling'

One of the most beautiful magnolias at San Francisco Botanical Garden, this cultivar flowers later than many other *Magnolia campbellii* cultivars and types. An Award of Garden Merit Winner in 2012.

SIZE AND HABIT 30 feet (9 m) tall and wide. Upright.
ZONES 7
FLOWERS Dark wine to purple-red and cup-and-saucer shaped; 7–12 inches (18–30 cm) across. Blooms late winter to early spring in San Francisco (Zone 10); mid- to late spring in England (Zones 8–9). Fragrant.
FOLIAGE Elliptic.
CULTIVATION Plant in sheltered spot to protect from the wind because of brittle branches and flowers. Full-sun with moist but well-drained soil. Propagate by cuttings or grafting.
ORIGIN Named by Hillier Nurseries, introduced by the Darjeeling Botanic Garden.

Magnolia champaca

yellow jade orchid tree
SYNONYM *Michelia champaca*

The flowers of this magnolia are used in the making of Jean Patou's Joy, a landmark floral perfume. On a warm night, you can smell the flowers from a considerable distance. Individual blossoms are often sold to perfume offices, cars, and homes. On a seed-collecting trip to Taiwan, our cab driver had one hanging from his visor.

SIZE AND HABIT 25–30 feet (8–9 m) tall and wide. Large shrub or small tree.
ZONES 9–10
FLOWERS Chromium yellow-orange; 2 inches (5 cm) across, with 12–14 tepals on axillary shoots. Blooms late spring to midsummer, and throughout most of the year. Extreme spiced perfume fragrance.
FOLIAGE Evergreen; bright green glossy leaves with undulating margin.
CULTIVATION Full sun to part shade. Propagate by seed or cuttings.
ORIGIN Native to southeastern Asia (China, India, Myanmar, Nepal, Vietnam).

Magnolia 'Cleopatra'

Small enough that it makes an ideal magnolia for a garden with limited space. It has shown high resistance to powdery mildew.

SIZE AND HABIT After ten years, 13 feet (4 m) tall, 6 feet (2 m) wide. Small, upright tree; broadly columnar.
ZONES 7a–8b
FLOWERS Red and purple, upright, and cup shaped; 7–8 inches (18–20 cm) across. Blooms early spring. Slight perfume fragrance.
FOLIAGE Slightly glossy.
FRUIT Attractive follicles in autumn.
CULTIVATION Full sun with soil rich in organic matter and some protection from the wind. Propagate by cuttings or grafting.
ORIGIN *Magnolia* ×*soulangeana* 'Sweet Simplicity' × *M.* 'Black Tulip', bred by Vance Hooper.

Magnolia 'Coral Lake'

While the parentage or 'Coral Lake' is thought to be primarily *Magnolia* 'Legend' and M. 'Butterflies', breeder David Leach speculated that some additional foreign pollen may be part of the genetic mix of this cultivar. While this is not a true yellow magnolia, it does have yellow tints suffused among the pink. And, like many other yellow-flowering magnolias, it blooms later and rarely runs the risk of being frosted. This is one of the most attractive magnolias at Scott Arboretum.

SIZE AND HABIT 32 feet (10 m) tall, 28 feet (9 m) wide. Upright, semi-fastigiate, slightly pyramidal, becoming broadly pyramidal over time.

ZONES 5–8

FLOWERS Peachy pink with vertical yellow stripes; upright, tulip shaped, and 7 inches (18 cm) across in full flower; with 11 tepals, 3–4 inches (8–10 cm) long. Blooms midspring. Pleasant fragrance.

FOLIAGE Obovate.

CULTIVATION Full sun with soil rich and high in organic matter. Propagate by cuttings or grafting.

ORIGIN *Magnolia* 'Legend × M. 'Butterflies', possibly with some pollen from *M. sprengeri* var. *diva* 'Diva', bred by David G. Leach and Curt Hanson.

Magnolia 'Daphne'

One of several great introductions from Arboretum Wespelaar in Belgium. Good yellow magnolia for a small garden. An Award of Garden Merit winner in 2012.

SIZE AND HABIT 8–12 feet (2–4 m) tall, 5–7 feet (2 m) wide. Large, compact shrub or small tree.
ZONES 5–9
FLOWERS Deep yellow; upright flowers on the tips of branches, with 9 sepals (3 yellowish green and 6 yellow). Blooms midspring.
FOLIAGE Elliptic.
CULTIVATION Full sun with well-drained soil. Propagate by cuttings or grafting.
ORIGIN *Magnolia acuminata* var. *subcordata* 'Miss Honeybee' × *M.* 'Gold Crown', bred by August Kehr, introduced by Arboretum Wespelaar.

Magnolia 'Dark Shadow'

The flowers of 'Dark Shadow' resemble those of the saucer magnolia, *Magnolia ×soulangeana*. It grows rapidly and flowers when young. Previously listed under the name 'JG 30'.

SIZE AND HABIT 25–30 feet (8–9 m) tall, 15 feet (5 m) wide. Compact tree.
ZONES 6–9
FLOWERS Reddish purple with nearly black-red buds. The chalice-shaped flowers open, revealing the white color on the inner tepal, which creates a dramatic contrast to the outer tepal. The stamens are also reddish purple. Blooms midspring.
FOLIAGE Ovate.
CULTIVATION Full sun with well-drained soil. Propagate by cuttings or grafting.
ORIGIN A Todd Gresham hybrid of unknown parentage, named by John Allen Smith.

Magnolia 'David Clulow'

Considered one of the best early white-flowering magnolias, and coveted by many gardeners. It has characteristics of *Magnolia campbellii*, but is far more tolerant of both cold and humidity. An Award of Garden Merit winner in 2012.

SIZE AND HABIT 22 feet (7 m) tall and wide. Broadly spreading.
ZONES 6–8
FLOWERS White, with a touch of pink at the base of the tepals; cup-and-saucer shaped and 8 inches (20 cm) across, with 12 tepals. Blooms early spring.
FOLIAGE Broadly ovate.
FRUIT Large follicles with ornamental appeal.
CULTIVATION Full sun with well-drained soil. Propagate by cuttings or grafting.
ORIGIN Unknown parentage; thought to be a hybrid between M. ×soulangeana 'Lennei Alba' and M. ×veitchii 'Rubra', bred by Ken Durio.

Magnolia dawsoniana
Dawson's magnolia

Named in honor of Jackson T. Dawson, superintendent of the Arnold Arboretum. Notable cultivars include 'Chyverton Red', with crimson-colored flowers, and 'Clarke', a deep pink, hardier form. Introduced by E. H. Wilson in 1908.

SIZE AND HABIT Up to 30 feet (9 m) tall and wide. Twiggy; more of a large shrub than a tree.
ZONES 6–8
FLOWERS White suffused with pinkish red; 10 inches (25 cm) across, with 9–12 tepals. After flowers open, they become limp and hang from the tree. Blooms early spring. Slight fragrance.
FOLIAGE Ovate; distinctive veining on upper and lower surfaces.
CULTIVATION Full sun with soil rich in organic matter. Propagate by seed, cuttings, or grafting.
ORIGIN Native to western Sichuan, China.

Magnolia 'Daybreak'

August Kehr considered this one of his finest introductions. Peak flowering in Tallahassee, Florida (Zone 8b), falls on the 17th of March. At the Holden Arboretum in Mentor, Ohio (Zone 6), it blooms for a three-week period. Because of its upright habit, it has been suggested as a replacement for *Pyrus calleryana*, callery pear, an overly used street tree with a host of problems. An Award of Garden Merit winner in 2012, and the recipient of a Gold Medal from the Pennsylvania Horticultural Society.

SIZE AND HABIT 40 feet (12 m) tall, 15 feet (5 m) wide. Medium sized, upright, fastigiate.
ZONES 5–8
FLOWERS Rose-pink; 9–10 inches (23–25 cm) across, with 8 splayed-out tepals. In bud they emerge with a slight green cast and then open to a suffusion of rose and pink. Darker on the outside of the tepals and lighter on the inside. Blooms midspring. Extremely fragrant.
FOLIAGE Elliptic.
CULTIVATION Full sun with well-drained soil. Propagate by cuttings or grafting.
ORIGIN *Magnolia ×brooklynensis* 'Woodsman' × M. 'Tina Durio', bred by August Kehr.

Magnolia delavayi
Delavay's magnolia

A species grown more for its foliage, Delavay's magnolia was introduced into England in 1899 by E. H. Wilson. The flowers appear sporadically and often occur at night, so there is never a considerable floral show. With protection, it can be grown as a wall plant.

SIZE AND HABIT 30 feet (9 m) tall and wide. Tree or large shrub; broad spreading.
ZONES 7b–9
FLOWERS Creamy white; 7 inches (18 cm) across, with 9 tepals. Blooms midsummer. Fragrant, most noticeably at night.
FOLIAGE Evergreen, ovate, and leathery; glaucous on underside.
CULTIVATION Full sun; tolerant of a wide range of soils, including chalky and acidic. Propagate by seed.
ORIGIN Native to Yunnan and southern Sichuan, China.

Magnolia denudata
Yulan magnolia

Of all the flowering magnolias at Scott Arboretum, this is one of the most beautiful, although it can be frosted every few years as a result of it's early blooming. In England it will bloom even earlier, in late winter to early spring. It is a parent of the highly ornamental saucer magnolia, *Magnolia ×soulangeana*. It is also known as the lily-tree or naked magnolia, because it blooms while the branches are still bare. An Award of Garden Merit winner in 1993.

SIZE AND HABIT 30–40 feet (9–12 m) tall and wide. Upright, but becoming more rounded and broad spreading with maturity. It can be cultivated as a single-trunked tree or with multiple stems.
ZONES 5–8
FLOWERS Creamy to ivory white, with 9–12 tepals. Upright and goblet shaped when borne, but opening as the flower ages. Tepals can have a tinge of pink or purple at the base. Blooms early spring. Lemon fragrance.
FOLIAGE Obovate.
FRUIT Follicles that eventually turn red.
CULTIVATION Full sun with well-drained soil. Good flowering will also occur in light shade. Grows in moist woodlands in its native habitat. Propagate by seed, cuttings, or grafting.
ORIGIN Native to Anhui, Zhejiang, Jiangxi, and Hunan, China.

Magnolia denudata 'Forrest's Pink'

A pink seedling of *Magnolia denudata* with good hardiness, but like the straight species it runs the risk of getting frosted in late winter to early spring.

SIZE AND HABIT 40 feet (12 m) tall and wide. Upright tree grown as a single-trunked or multi-stemmed tree and pyramidal when young.

ZONES 5–8

FLOWERS Clear bubble gum pink, flushed with deeper pink at the base of the tepal; 4–8 inches (10–20 cm) across, with 9–11 tepals. Blooms early spring. Fragrant.

FOLIAGE Obovate.

FRUIT Follicles that eventually turn red.

CULTIVATION Full sun with well-drained soil. Propagate by cuttings or grafting.

ORIGIN Bred by Treseder's Nurseries.

Magnolia denudata 'Swarthmore Sentinel'

J. C. Raulston donated this seedling of *Magnolia denudata* to Scott Arboretum in 1993 from seed that he had received from the Beijing Botanic Garden. From a very young age, the plant exhibited a very narrow and upright habit. The arboretum eventually registered it with the Magnolia Society International in 2009.

SIZE AND HABIT After 20 years, 40 feet (12 m) tall, 15 feet (5 m) wide. Upright, strictly pyramidal.

ZONES 5–9

FLOWERS Creamy to ivory white, with 9–12 tepals. Upright and goblet shaped when borne, but opening as the flower ages. Tepals can have a tinge of pink or purple at the base. Blooms early spring. Fragrant.

FOLIAGE Elliptic to obovate.

FRUIT Follicles that eventually turn red.

CULTIVATION Full sun with well-drained soil. Propagate by cuttings or grafting.

ORIGIN Named by Scott Arboretum of Swarthmore College. Seed came from J. C. Raulston in 1993; he obtained it from Beijing Botanical Garden.

Magnolia doltsopa

sweet michelia

SYNONYMS *Michelia excelsa, Michelia doltsopa*

Effective as a street tree or pruned into hedges, sweet michelia typically starts flowering in mid-winter. A wonderful specimen can be found at San Francisco Botanical Garden. 'Silver Cloud' is a compact small tree with pyramidal or conical habit. It can be used in a small garden and is good for hedging.

SIZE AND HABIT Up to 35 feet (11 m) tall in cultivation, and up to 100 feet (30 m) tall in the wild; 35–50 feet (11–15 m) wide. Upright tree; conical to oval.

ZONES 9–11

FLOWERS Pure white; 5–7 inches (13–18 cm) across, with 12 tepals. Fuzzy brown buds are large and attractive. Blooms midwinter to early spring. Strong fragrance.

FOLIAGE Evergreen; glossy dark green.

CULTIVATION Sheltered position in full sun to part shade with well-drained soil. Propagate by seed or cuttings.

ORIGIN Native to the Himalayas (Nepal, Bhutan, India, northern Myanmar, India [Assam], China).

Magnolia 'Elizabeth'

This hybrid was named in honor of Elizabeth van Brunt, a patron of Brooklyn Botanic Garden. The soft yellow flowers can be more intense in areas with stronger light, such as New Zealand. Blooms in early to midspring in St. Louis, Missouri (Zone 6); flowering can last for up to four weeks. Bark can be susceptible to frost cracks in some winters. This was one of the very first yellow magnolias to be introduced; many more recent yellow selections have more intense flowers. Selected as a Great Plant Picks for Northwest gardens, an Award of Garden Merit winner in 1993, and the recipient of a Gold Medal from the Pennsylvania Horticultural Society.

SIZE AND HABIT 30–50 feet (9–15 m) tall, 20–25 feet (6–8 m) wide. Upright, pyramidal, multi-stemmed tree.

ZONES 5–8

FLOWERS Clear primrose yellow and upward facing with long, tapering buds; 8 inches (20 cm) across, with 6–9 tepals. Flowers open up as they mature revealing red stamens. Blooms midspring. Fragrant.

FOLIAGE Young emerging leaves are copper colored and obovate.

CULTIVATION Full sun with well-drained soil. Propagate by cuttings or grafting.

ORIGIN *Magnolia acuminata* × *M. denudata*, bred by Eva Maria Sperber.

Magnolia 'Eternal Spring'

'Eternal Spring' has a long bloom period (up to three to four weeks) from early to midspring, though once at the originator's garden, Camellia Forest Nursery, North Carolina (Zone 7b), they had a heavy bloom in early autumn.

SIZE AND HABIT 20 feet (6 m) tall, 15 feet (5 m) wide. Small tree.
ZONES 7–9
FLOWERS White; 3 inches (8 cm) across, with 10 tepals. Blooms early spring. Fragrant.
FOLIAGE Evergreen.
CULTIVATION Partial winter shade with well-drained soil. Propagate by cuttings.
ORIGIN *Magnolia laevifolia* × *M. maudiae*, bred by Camellia Forest Nursery.

Magnolia 'Exotic Star'

A new and very interesting evergreen hybrid that combines the large summer flowers of *Magnolia grandiflora* with the distinctive showy stamens of *M. sieboldii*. Flowering can occur repeatedly throughout summer. It is vigorous and blooms at a young age. 'Exotic Star', with its upright habit, is a superb choice for areas with limited space.

SIZE AND HABIT 30 feet (9 m) tall, 25 feet (8 m) wide. Very narrow and upright.
ZONES 6
FLOWERS *Magnolia grandiflora*–like flowers, 4–5 inches (10–13 cm) across, with orange-red stamens and up to 16 tepals that are pure white. Blooms midsummer. Sweet fragrance, similar to *M. grandiflora*.
FOLIAGE Glossy and evergreen, with indumentum on underside of leaves, similar to its parent, *M. grandiflora* 'Russet'.
CULTIVATION Sun to part shade with well-drained soils. Propagate by cuttings.
ORIGIN *Magnolia sieboldii* × *M. grandiflora* 'Russet', bred by Dennis Ledvina.

Magnolia Fairy Cream 'MicJur2'

A member of the Fairy Magnolia series along with Fairy Blush and Fairy White. In colder winters or temperatures, many of the evergreen leaves may shed. A popular cultivar in New Zealand, Australia, California and the southeastern United States.

SIZE AND HABIT After seven years, 9–12 feet (3–4 m) tall, 7–9 feet (2–3 m) wide, but can be kept to any size with pruning. Shrublike, compact.

ZONES 7b–11

FLOWERS Creamy flowers, 2.5 inches (6 cm) across, opening from brown velvety buds. Flowers are borne along the stem, producing a more significant floral show. Blooms early to midspring, with sporadic rebloom in summer and autumn. Sweet fragrance.

FOLIAGE Evergreen.

CULTIVATION Can be used for hedging and screening. Full sun to part shade with moist but well-drained soil. For a hedge, plant specimens 3–4 feet (1 m) apart. Propagate by cuttings.

ORIGIN *Magnolia figo* × (*M. doltsopa* × *M. yuyuanensis*), bred by Mark Jury.

Magnolia Felix 'JURmag2'

Felix has complex parentage. One parent, *Magnolia* 'Vulcan', is a sister seedling of 'Apollo', which resulted from a cross between *M. campbellii* subsp. *mollicomata* 'Lanarth' and *M. liliiflora*. The other, 'Atlas', is a hybrid between *M. ×soulangeana* 'Lennei' and *M.* 'Mark Jury'. The result of this complex parentage is a large water lily–like flower with attributes of *M. campbellii*, *M. liliiflora*, and the saucer magnolia, *M. ×soulangeana*. Felix is named for Felix Jury, Mark Jury's father and famed magnolia breeder from New Zealand. It blooms from mid- to late spring, lasting up to three weeks. An Award of Garden Merit winner in 2013.

SIZE AND HABIT 16 feet (5 m) tall, 11 feet (3 m) wide. Small, upright, pyramidal tree.

ZONES 5b–9

FLOWERS Deep rose-red, water lily–like flowers, 12 inches (30 cm) across. Blooms midspring. Extremely fragrant.

FOLIAGE Light green.

CULTIVATION Full sun with well-drained soil. Propagate by cuttings or grafting.

ORIGIN *Magnolia* 'Atlas' × *M.* 'Vulcan', bred by Mark Jury.

Magnolia figo

banana shrub
SYNONYM *Michelia figo*

Magnolia figo is excellent for hedging, screening, or used as a foundation plant. It can be grown successfully in the US Southeast and South, as well as in California and the Pacific Northwest (Zones 8–10). In Tallahassee, Florida (Zone 8b), it blooms in early to midspring for up to six weeks. 'Port Wine' has purple-tinged flowers and can bloom for up to four to six weeks. *Magnolia figo* var. *crassipes* 'Purple Queen' has deep red-purple flowers edged in white.

SIZE AND HABIT 10–20 feet (3–6 m) tall, 6–15 feet (2–5 m) wide. Shrubby, multi-stemmed, pyramidal. It can be pruned into a topiary or espalier.
ZONE 8–10
FLOWERS Fuzzy buds opening to a creamy yellow; 1.5 inches (4 cm) across, with 6–9 upward-facing tepals edged or streaked with purple at the base. Blooms early to midspring. Banana fragrance.
FOLIAGE Evergreen, glossy, and ovate. Covered in brown pubescence when emerging.
CULTIVATION Full sun to part shade with well-drained soil. It can tolerate both acid and alkaline soils. Good for screening or hedging. It can be prone to scale infestations, which can defoliate the plant. Propagate by cuttings.
ORIGIN Native to China.

Magnolia ×*foggii* 'Jack Fogg'

Jack Fogg banana shrub

SYNONYM *Michelia* ×*foggii* 'Jack Fogg'

This magnolia can be grown as a loose shrub or pruned into a hedge and is most popular on the US West Coast or in southeastern states. 'Allspice' is a clone with large white flowers and a strong fragrance.

SIZE AND HABIT 15 feet (5 m) tall and wide. Narrow.
ZONES 7a–9b
FLOWERS White and pinkish purple on the edges; 5 inches (13 cm) across. Borne throughout the branches. Attractive buds covered in brown indumentum. Blooms early spring. Banana fragrance.
FOLIAGE Leaves are small, evergreen, and glossy green.
CULTIVATION Sun to part-shade with well-drained soil and some protection from the wind.
ORIGIN *Magnolia figo* × *M. doltsopa*, bred by John M. Fogg. Propagate by cuttings.

Magnolia foveolata 'Shibamichi'

Guangdong gardenia
SYNONYM *Michelia foveolata*

Blooming as early as late winter in Raleigh, North Carolina (Zone 8), Guangdong gardenia generally blooms in midspring in Zones 7b–8a, though it can also send out a flush of flowers in late summer. Hardy in Vancouver, British Columbia (Zones 8–9).

SIZE AND HABIT 30 feet (9 m) tall, 18 feet (5 m) wide. Upright, fairly open habit.
ZONES 7–10
FLOWERS Creamy yellow with red anthers; 2.5–4 inches (6–10 cm) across. Flowers are globe-like, opening to cup shaped. Blooms late winter to early spring. Very mild fragrance, reminiscent of canned pears.
FOLIAGE Evergreen, with attractive golden indumentum on underside of leaves.
CULTIVATION Sun to part shade. Young plants must be irrigated during periods of drought. Propagate by cuttings and seed (straight species). Graft easily onto *Michelia*-type species and *Magnolia kobus*.
ORIGIN Selected by Akira Shibamichi, Shibamichi Nursery, Saitama, Japan.

Magnolia 'Frank's Masterpiece'

A red, upright magnolia with very large flowers and good vigor.

SIZE AND HABIT 30 feet (9 m) tall, 25 feet (8 m) wide. Strong leader with slight weeping to pyramidal habit.

ZONES 5–9

FLOWERS 10–11 inches (25–28 cm) across, with 8–9 tepals. Tepals are 5 inches (13 cm) long and 4 inches (10 cm) wide. The outer tepal is a striking reddish purple and the inner tepal white with a pink blush. Blooms early spring.

FOLIAGE Elliptic.

CULTIVATION Full sun. Propagate by cuttings or grafting.

ORIGIN *Magnolia* ×*soulangeana* 'Deep Purple Dream' × *M*. 'Paul Cook', bred by Frank Gaylon.

Magnolia fraseri

Fraser magnolia

One of a handful of large-leaf native magnolias that can be grown for a bold textural effect in the garden. Other American magnolias with outstanding large deciduous leaves include *Magnolia macrophylla*, *M. macrophylla* subsp. *ashei*, and *M. tripetala*. For a deciduous magnolia, Fraser magnolia has good yellow autumn color.

SIZE AND HABIT 30–60 feet (9–18 m) tall, 20–30 feet (6–9 m) wide. Often a multi-stemmed tree.
ZONES 5b–9
FLOWERS Creamy white and vase shaped, becoming open faced; up to 12 inches (30 cm) across, with 9 tepals. Blooms midspring. Slight fragrance.
FOLIAGE Rhombic (kite shaped), with an auriculate leaf base like *M. macrophylla* and *M. macrophylla* subsp. *ashei*.
FRUIT Rose-red at maturity.
CULTIVATION Prefers moist woodlands in the wild, but in cultivation can grow in full sun to part shade with moist soil. Propagate by seed.
ORIGIN Native to the southern Appalachian Mountains from Virginia to Kentucky and to Georgia and Alabama.

Magnolia 'Galaxy'

As a result of its single-stemmed, upright habit and oval canopy, I have seen 'Galaxy' used effectively as a street tree in a parking lot on the Ohio State University campus. It flowers late enough that it rarely gets frost damage. It has the same parentage as *Magnolia* 'Spectrum'. An Award of Garden Merit winner in 1993.

SIZE AND HABIT 30 feet (9 m) tall, 20–25 feet (6–8 m) wide. Single-stemmed, upright tree with a distinct oval canopy.
ZONES 4a–8
FLOWERS Deep reddish purple in bud, opening to lighter pinkish purple on the inner tepal; 8–10 inches (20–25 cm) across, with 12 tepals. Blooms midspring. Slight fragrance.
FOLIAGE Ovate.
CULTIVATION Full sun with well-drained soil. It is very adaptable to poor soils. Propagate by cuttings or grafting.
ORIGIN *Magnolia liliiflora* 'Nigra' × *M. sprengeri* var. *diva* 'Diva', bred by William Kosar, introduced by Frank Santamour, Jr.

Magnolia 'Genie'

A great magnolia for the small garden. Blooms most vigorously in spring, followed by sporadic flowering thereafter. Considered to be a red magnolia due to its black-red flowers.

SIZE AND HABIT 13 feet (4 m) tall, 5–6 feet (2 m) wide. Compact, small tree with pyramidal shape.

ZONES 4–9

FLOWERS Maroon to magenta; 6 inches (15 cm) wide, with 6–12 tepals. Open tulip shape, becoming more gobletlike as they unfurl. The outer and inner tepals both have the same strong coloring. Blooms midspring. Fragrant.

FOLIAGE Ovate.

CULTIVATION Full sun with well-drained soil. Propagate by cuttings or grafting.

ORIGIN *Magnolia* 'Sweet Valentine' × (*M. ×soulangeana* 'Sweet Simplicity' × *M. liliiflora* 'Nigra'), bred by Vance Hooper.

Magnolia grandiflora 'Bracken's Brown Beauty'

This is a very cold-hardy magnolia that has withstood temperatures as low as −20°F (−29°C). Because of its stature it can be used for hedging, topiary, and as a residential street tree. The brown indumentum on the underside of the leaves gives this an added ornamental attribute. Recipient of the Gold Medal from the Pennsylvania Horticultural Society.

SIZE AND HABIT 30–50 feet (9–15 m) tall, 15–30 feet (5–9 m) wide. Densely pyramidal to oval.
ZONES 5b–9
FLOWERS Creamy white; 5–6 inches (13–15 cm) across. Flowers are half the size of the straight species and some other cultivars. Blooms late spring to midsummer. Lemon fragrance.
FOLIAGE Dark, lustrous green, with striking brown indumentum on the underside. Leaves have an undulating margin.
CULTIVATION Full sun to part shade with well-drained soil. Propagate by cuttings.
ORIGIN Selected by Ray Bracken.

Magnolia grandiflora 'Claudia Wannamaker'

An early cultivar in the trade introduced in 1956 in the southeastern United States. The foliage and flowers are smaller than many forms and selections, thus giving it a more refined appearance, and it flowers at a young age. It has a more open habit than 'Bracken's Brown Beauty'. In Zones 8–9, it starts flowering in late spring and continues into early autumn.

SIZE AND HABIT 50–60 feet (15–18 m) tall, 20–30 feet (6–9 m) wide. Broadly pyramidal; dense and uniform habit.
ZONES 7–10
FLOWERS Creamy white; 3–4 inches (8–10 cm) across. Blooms late spring to midsummer. Lemon fragrance.
FOLIAGE With striking brown indumentum on the underside.
CULTIVATION Full sun to part shade with well-drained soil. Propagate by cuttings.
ORIGIN Selected by John F. Brailsford, Sr., Shady Grove Nursery.

Magnolia 'Heaven Scent'

A good substitute for *Magnolia* ×*soulangeana*. Similar in stature to many of the other Todd Gresham hybrids. An Award of Garden Merit winner in 1993.

SIZE AND HABIT 26–39 feet (8–12 m) tall and wide. Broadly rounded.
ZONES 5–8
FLOWERS Rose-purple and tulip to goblet shaped; 4 inches (10 cm) across, with 9 rosy pink tepals that fade to pink with a magenta stripe at the base of the tepals. Flowers open up and splay open. Blooms midspring. Fragrant.
FOLIAGE Elliptic.
CULTIVATION Sun to part shade. Propagate by cuttings or grafting.
ORIGIN *Magnolia liliiflora* 'Nigra' × *M.* ×*veitchii*, bred by Todd Gresham.

Magnolia 'Holland Rose'

This is a relatively small cultivar, making it perfect for the small garden. A recent introduction, it flowers profusely and has good hardiness.

SIZE AND HABIT After ten years, 7 feet (2 m) tall, 5 feet (2 m) wide. Large, multi-stemmed shrub.

ZONES 4–8

FLOWERS Tulip shaped and upward facing, with 6 tepals. Red-purple striping on the outer tepals; inner tepals are white. Blooms midspring. Fragrant.

FOLIAGE Elliptic.

CULTIVATION Full sun with well-drained soil. Propagate by cuttings or grafting.

ORIGIN *Magnolia liliiflora* 'Holland Red' × *M.* ×*loebneri* 'White Rose', bred by Dennis Ledvina and Roy Klehm.

Magnolia Honey Tulip 'JURmag5'

This Mark Jury selection flowers earlier than most of the yellow magnolias. A new introduction from the Jury magnolia breeding program in New Zealand, it is a great yellow magnolia for small gardens.

SIZE AND HABIT 12 feet (4 m) tall, 13 feet (4 m) wide. Small flowering tree, more upright than broad spreading.
ZONES 7
FLOWERS Soft yellow and goblet shaped. Blooms early spring.
FOLIAGE Elliptic.
CULTIVATION Full sun to part shade with well-drained soil. Propagate by cuttings or grafting.
ORIGIN Bred by Mark Jury.

Magnolia insignis

red lotus tree
SYNONYM *Manglietia insignis*

Red lotus tree has been gaining popularity as one of the best evergreen magnolias for the temperate climate of the Pacific Northwest, so much so that it is being used as a breeding parent with many other species of magnolias. It starts flowering from late spring into summer. A very heavy bloomer, flowers are produced sporadically for several weeks and last two to three days. Occasionally, there will be a few blooms in early autumn. The buds are also ornamental. They are red in color and stand erect like candles before opening. 'Anita Figlar', selected by Richard Figlar and named for his wife, is more profuse than straight *Magnolia insignis*. It has 9 tepals in three tiers of 3 tepals, each with the outer 3 tepals reflexing downward. The inner tier is a deep red on both sides of the tepal. The smaller inner tepal is pale pink to white. This creates a bicolored effect up close, but from afar the flowers look red.

SIZE AND HABIT 25 feet (8 m) tall, 20 feet (6 m) wide, but up to 100 feet (30 m) tall in the wild. Upright, pyramidal.

ZONES 7a–9

FLOWERS Creamy white to pink to scarlet, depending on the form; 6 inches (15 cm) across, with 9–12 tepals. The pink form is white at the base, fading to white and pink and all pink at the tips of the tepals. Flowers are upright and open faced. Blooms late spring to midsummer. Fragrant.

FOLIAGE Evergreen and ovate to elliptic; glossy dark green.

CULTIVATION Part shade with moist soil. Propagate by seed or cuttings.

ORIGIN Native to southern China across Yunnan and northern Vietnam, Myanmar, and northeast India west to Nepal.

Magnolia 'Iolanthe'

'Iolanthe' flowers from mid- to late winter in regions with milder winters and late spring in colder climates.

SIZE AND HABIT 25 feet (8 m) tall, 20 feet (6 m) wide. Fast growing with a strong leader.
ZONES 6–9
FLOWERS The large cup-and-saucer-shaped *M. campbellii*–like flowers are 11 inches (28 cm) across, with 9 large tepals. Tepals are clear pink on the outside and white inside, creating a bicolored effect. Blooms mid- to late winter.
FOLIAGE Elliptic.
CULTIVATION Full sun with some protection from the wind. Propagate by cuttings or grafting.
ORIGIN *Magnolia* ×*soulangeana* 'Lennei' × *M.* 'Mark Jury', bred by Felix Jury.

Magnolia 'Ivory Chalice'

While this has the parentage of many of the yellow hybrids, the flowers are more like those of *Magnolia denudata* in that they are a beautiful creamy white. A very hardy cultivar that can survive temperatures as low as −22°F (−30°C).

SIZE AND HABIT 30 feet (9 m) tall, 16 feet (5 m) wide. Very upright to pyramidal with an oval canopy.
ZONES 4
FLOWERS 6 inches (15 cm) across, with 9 creamy yellow tepals tipped with narrow stripes of reddish purple. Blooms early spring.
FOLIAGE Obovate.
CULTIVATION Full sun with well-drained soil. Propagate by cuttings or grafting.
ORIGIN *Magnolia acuminata* × *M. denudata*, bred by David Leach.

Magnolia 'Jane'

Another member of The Girls series, 'Jane' blooms later than *Magnolia stellata* and *M. ×soulangeana* and has a more diminutive habit.

SIZE AND HABIT 10–15 feet (3–5 m) tall, 8–12 feet (2–4 m) wide. Broadly rounded, forming a compact, upright shrub.

ZONES 4–9

FLOWERS Cup shaped, 3–4 inches (8–10 cm) across, with 8–10 tepals. Tepals are red-purple on the outside and white on the inside. Blooming can occur sporadically throughout the season. Blooms midspring. Fragrant.

FOLIAGE Ovate.

CULTIVATION Full sun with well-drained soil. Propagate by cuttings or grafting.

ORIGIN *Magnolia liliiflora* 'Reflorescens' × *M. stellata* 'Waterlily', bred by William Kosar and Francis de Vos.

Magnolia 'Jon Jon'

SYNONYM *Magnolia* 'JG#3'

'Jon Jon' blooms later than many early magnolias (two weeks after saucer magnolias) and therefore avoids getting frosted in most years. It flowers profusely from late winter to early spring in Zone 8b and midspring in Zone 7a. Selected by John Allen Smith from Todd Gresham hybrids planted at Gloster Arboretum in Mississippi.

SIZE AND HABIT 30 feet (9 m) tall, 15 feet (5 m) wide. Upright with a rounded canopy.
ZONES 6b–9a
FLOWERS Goblet shaped, up to 12 inches (30 cm) across, opening to platelike blooms; 9 broad, white tepals, 5.5–6 inches (14–15 cm) long, with rose-pink coloration at the base. Blooms early spring. Fragrant.
FOLIAGE Obovate.
CULTIVATION Full sun to part shade. Propagate by cuttings or grafting.
ORIGIN Unknown parentage; most likely *M.* ×*soulangeana* × *M.* ×*veitchii*, bred by John Allen Smith.

Magnolia '**Judy Zuk**'

Named in honor of the former president of Brooklyn Botanic Garden, this upright yellow magnolia is perfect for spaces where a narrow plant is needed. It is a favorite at Scott Arboretum for its stature, colorful flowers, and fruity fragrance. For many years this was an unnamed clone under the designation BBGRC 1164.

SIZE AND HABIT 20 feet (6 m) tall, 18 feet (5 m) wide. Upright, especially when young. The canopy broadens out slightly with age, becoming more oval to rounded.

ZONES 4–9

FLOWERS Gold-orange or -yellow and tulip shaped, with rose-pink blush at the base; 5 inches (13 cm) across, but very upright. Blooms midspring. Fruity fragrance.

FOLIAGE Ovate.

CULTIVATION Full sun with well-drained soil. Propagate by cuttings or grafting.

ORIGIN *Magnolia acuminata* × (*M. liliiflora* × *M. stellata*), bred by Brooklyn Botanic Garden.

Magnolia 'Katie-O Early'

'Katie-O Early' represents a breakthrough in magnolia hybridizing: it is the first evergreen-to-semi-evergreen hardy tree for Zone 7 with flower colors other than white.

SIZE AND HABIT Most likely 30 feet (9 m) tall, 20 feet (6 m) wide at maturity. Upright tree with slightly spreading habit.

ZONES 7–9

FLOWERS Pink and goblet shaped; 4 inches (10 cm) across, with 11 tepals. Tepals are soft pink and upward facing. Flowers are waterlilylike and similar in size and shape to those of *M. virginiana* var. *australis*. Blooms May to June. Fragrant.

FOLIAGE Evergreen, *M. virginiana*–like leaves, but only slightly glaucous on underside.

CULTIVATION Part shade to full sun. Due to the *Magnolia virginiana* var. *australis* parentage, it may be tolerant of moist soils. Propagate by grafting.

ORIGIN *Magnolia insignis* × *M. virginiana* var. *australis*, bred by S. Christopher Early.

Magnolia ×kewensis 'Wada's Memory'

This is a very floriferous tree and one of the best early spring–flowering magnolias at Scott Arboretum. It has good vigor and blooms at a young age. Named in honor of Japanese nurseryman Koichiro Wada.

SIZE AND HABIT 40 feet (12 m) tall, 30 feet (9 m) wide. Single- or multi-stemmed tree. Upright and pyramidal when young, broadening out over time.

ZONES 5a–8b

FLOWERS White, upward facing, and tulip shaped; 7 inches (18 cm) across, with 6 long tepals. Flowers eventually open up all the way and droop at the tips, making for a dramatic display. Blooms early spring. Fragrant.

FOLIAGE Elliptic; bronze in color as the foliage unfurls.

CULTIVATION Full sun with well-drained soil. Propagate by cuttings or grafting.

ORIGIN *Magnolia kobus* × *M. salicifolia*, bred by Brian Mulligan.

Magnolia kobus
Kobus magnolia

A tall, upright species, Kobus magnolia is basically a tree version of *Magnolia stellata* or *M. ×loebneri*. The flowers can be frost sensitive due to flowering so early in the season. Used as the understock for grafting many species and cultivars of magnolias due to the consistent vigor, quality, and uniformity of the seedlings.

SIZE AND HABIT 30–40 feet (9–12 m) tall, but sometimes up to 80 feet (24 m) in the wild; 20–25 feet (6–8 m) wide. Very upright with a single trunk (though sometimes multi-stemmed).

ZONES 4–8

FLOWERS White, sometimes pink; 4 inches (10 cm) across, with 9–12 tepals. Winter buds are very fuzzy and attractive. Blooms early spring. Fragrant.

FOLIAGE Obovate.

CULTIVATION Full sun with well-drained soil; will tolerate many soil types including limestone. Propagate by seed or cuttings.

ORIGIN Native to Japan and South Korea.

Magnolia laevifolia

michelia

Formerly known as *Michelia yunnanensis* and *Magnolia dianica*. A great magnolia for small gardens, michelia can be maintained as a hedge or a foundation planting. It is a good landscape plant in Belgium and the Netherlands, where winters are not extreme. Flowering can start as early as midwinter and continue into autumn depending on the location. 'Strybing Compact' is a good compact form. 'Copperstop' has fury stems and leaves with coppery undersides, giving this cultivar its name. 'Michelle' is a profuse-flowering cultivar that is 18 feet (5 m) tall and 10 feet (3 m) wide and has good form. 'Snowbird' is more diminutive at 6 feet (2 m) tall and 4 feet (1 m) wide, making it perfect for foundation plantings and hedges. Other cultivars include 'Inspiration' and 'Free Spirit'.

SIZE AND HABIT 18 feet (5 m) tall, 10 feet (3 m) wide. Small tree or large shrub with cinnamon indumentum on buds. Unlike other magnolias, the buds form in the axils of the leaves along the stems, thus producing a more profuse look.

ZONES 7b–10b

FLOWERS Ivory white and chalice shaped; 4 inches (10 cm) across, with a boss of striking yellow stamens made up of 6–12 tepals. Blooms midwinter to autumn. Lemon fragrance.

FOLIAGE Evergreen and oval shaped, with golden edge. Slight indumentum on underside.

FRUIT Prolific; can be attractive.

CULTIVATION Sun to part shade with well-drained soil; tolerant of lime soils. Propagate by seed or cuttings.

ORIGIN Native to Yunnan, Guizhou, and Sichuan, China.

Magnolia liliiflora 'Nigra'

lily magnolia

An important parent to many magnolias, including The Girls series, and the 'Galaxy', 'Marillyn', and 'Spectrum' hybrids. An Award of Garden Merit winner in 1993.

SIZE AND HABIT 15 feet (5 m) tall, 12 feet (4 m) wide. Large deciduous shrub to a small flowering tree with a rounded habit.

ZONES 6–9

FLOWERS Dark purple and vase shaped; 4–5 inches (10–13 cm) across, with 9–18 tepals. Blooms midspring. Slight fragrance.

FOLIAGE Elliptic to ovate.

CULTIVATION Full sun with well-drained soil. Propagate by cuttings or grafting.

ORIGIN Bred by Veitch Nursery. It is thought that there are no true plants left in the wild with the exception of escaped or naturalized plants.

Magnolia ×*loebneri* 'Ballerina'

Loebner magnolia

In Zone 7, *Magnolia* ×*loebneri* flowers slightly later than *M. stellata, M. kobus, M.* ×*soulangeana, M. salicifolia,* and *M. denudata,* but it does still flower early enough to be vulnerable to spring frosts. There are many cultivars. 'Ballerina' is slightly smaller and grows more slowly than 'Merrill'.

SIZE AND HABIT 15–20 feet (5–6 m) tall and wide. Upright in youth, becoming broadly rounded with age.
ZONES 5–9
FLOWERS White; 2–3 inches (5–8 cm) long, with a profusion of 30 tepals. Tepals have a pale pink flush at the base. Blooms early spring, later than many *M.* ×*loebneri* cultivars. Strong fragrance.
FOLIAGE Green and obovate.
CULTIVATION Full sun with well-drained soil. Propagate by cuttings or grafting.
ORIGIN *Magnolia* ×*loebneri* 'Spring Snow' × (possibly) *M. stellata* 'Waterlily', bred by J. C. McDaniel.

Magnolia ×loebneri 'Donna'

Named for breeder Harry Heineman's wife, this selection was made in Boston, Massachusetts (Zone 6), and has proven hardiness. An Award of Garden Merit winner in 2012.

SIZE AND HABIT 15 feet (5 m) tall, 12 feet (4 m) wide. Upright, densely branched shrub.
ZONES 5–9
FLOWERS Pure white; 6–7 inches (15–18 cm) across, with 12–13 broad, reflexed tepals. Larger and flatter than those of most *M. ×loebneri* cultivars. Blooms early spring. Fragrant.
FOLIAGE Narrowly elliptic.
CULTIVATION Full sun with well-drained soil. Propagate by cuttings or grafting.
ORIGIN A hybrid involving *M. stellata*, bred by Harry Heineman.

Magnolia ×loebneri 'Leonard Messel'

One of the top ten magnolias at Scott Arboretum. The flowers are very frost resistant and it blooms later than the earliest magnolias. An Award of Garden Merit winner in 1993.

SIZE AND HABIT 15–20 feet (5–6 m) tall, 20–25 feet (6–8 m) wide. Large shrub or small tree, becoming rounded with age.

ZONES 5–9

FLOWERS Purple in bud, opening to deep pink with a slight white tinge on insides of tepals; 5 inches (13 cm) across, with 12 linear tepals, 3 inches (8 cm) long. Inner tepals are slightly lighter pink than outer tepals. Blooms early spring. Fragrant.

FOLIAGE Narrowly elliptic.

CULTIVATION Full sun with well-drained soil. Propagate by cuttings or grafting.

ORIGIN *Magnolia kobus* × *M. stellata* 'Rosea', bred by Leonard Messel.

Magnolia ×loebneri 'Mag's Pirouette'

An Award of Garden Merit winner in 2012.

SIZE AND HABIT 12 feet (4 m) tall and wide. Upright.
ZONES 5–9
FLOWERS Small and white; 4 inches (10 cm) across, with many tepals. Outer tepals are shorter than the inner tepals. Blooms early spring. Fragrant.
FOLIAGE Narrowly elliptic.
CULTIVATION Full sun with well-drained soil. Propagate by cuttings or grafting.
ORIGIN Seedling of *M. ×loebneri* 'Ballerina', bred by Tetsuo Magaki.

Magnolia ×loebneri 'Merrill'

A very floriferous and vigorous cultivar. Hardy in even some of the coldest parts of Minnesota and Maine. It is named for Elmer Drew Merrill, former director of the Arnold Arboretum at Harvard University. An Award of Garden Merit winner in 1993.

SIZE AND HABIT 30 feet (9 m) tall and wide. Many branched and low to the ground with an upright canopy and an oval form. Vigorous and fast growing.

ZONES 3b–8

FLOWERS Large and white, with 15 broad tepals that are 4–6 inches (10–15 cm) wide. Blooms early spring. Fragrant.

FOLIAGE Narrowly elliptic.

CULTIVATION Full sun with well-drained soil. Propagate by cuttings or grafting.

ORIGIN Bred by Karl Sax.

Magnolia ×*loebneri* 'Spring Snow'

This is a good cold-hardy cultivar; flowers are rarely damaged by snow or cold weather. It flowers later than other *Magnolia* ×*loebneri* cultivars.

SIZE AND HABIT 25–30 feet (8–9 m) tall and wide. Rounded.
ZONE 5–8
FLOWERS Pure white; 3 inches (8 cm) wide, with 15–20 tepals. Blooms early spring. Fragrant.
FOLIAGE Narrowly elliptic.
CULTIVATION Full sun with well-drained soil; can tolerate fairly cold temperatures. Propagate by cuttings or grafting.
ORIGIN Bred by J. C. McDaniel.

Magnolia ×loebneri 'White Rose'

Yet another good cold-hardy *Magnolia ×loebneri* cultivar.

SIZE AND HABIT 20 feet (6 m) tall, 15 feet (5 m) wide. Smaller, rounded stature than some other *M. ×loebneri* cultivars.
ZONES 4–8
FLOWERS White; 2–2.5 inches (5–6 cm) across, with 22 tepals, 1.5 inches (4 cm) long. Flowers can be slightly purple on the mid-rib and base of the tepals. Flower form is reminiscent of a white gardenia or rose with erect, firm, and perky tepals. Blooms early spring. Sweet fragrance.
FOLIAGE Narrowly elliptic.
CULTIVATION Full sun with well-drained soil. Propagate by cuttings or grafting.
ORIGIN Seedling of *M. ×loebneri* 'Ballerina', bred by W. J. Siedl (Manitowoc, Wisconsin).

Magnolia ×*loebneri* 'Wildcat'

'Wildcat' flowers over a six-week period at the same time as many other M. ×*loebneri* cultivars. The flowers look white from a distance, but closer inspection reveals a soft pink blush. While these are typically grown as multi-stemmed trees, they can also make a nice single-trunked option. An Award of Garden Merit winner in 2012.

SIZE AND HABIT 18 feet (5 m) tall, 8–12 feet (2–4 m) wide. Large bush or small tree; upright.
ZONES 5–8
FLOWERS Soft pink and chrysanthemumlike; 4–5 inches (10–13 cm) across, with an amazing 52 tepals. Blooms early spring. Slight fragrance.
FOLIAGE Narrowly elliptic.
CULTIVATION Full sun with well-drained soil. Propagate by cuttings or grafting.
ORIGIN Seedling of M. *kobus* var. *borealis*, selected by Larry Langford.

Magnolia 'Lois'

An introduction from Brooklyn Botanic Garden named in honor of former chairman of the board of directors Lois Carswell, this cultivar is very similar to *Magnolia* 'Elizabeth', but the flower color is a deeper yellow and it flowers slightly later, just before the leaves emerge. It stays more diminutive in size than some of the other yellows. It has a nice stout form in its youth. An Award of Garden Merit winner in 2012.

SIZE AND HABIT 15–20 feet (5–6 m) tall, 18 feet (5 m) wide. Small tree with a rounded canopy.
ZONES 5–8b
FLOWERS Sulfur yellow, upright, and goblet shaped; 5 inches (13 cm) across. Blooms midspring. Slight fragrance.
FOLIAGE Broadly elliptic.
CULTIVATION Full sun with well-drained soil. Propagate by cuttings or grafting.
ORIGIN *Magnolia acuminata* × (*M. acuminata* × *M. denudata*), bred by Lola Koerting.

Magnolia lotungensis

eastern joy lotus tree
SYNONYM *Parakmeria lotungensis*

The eastern joy lotus tree has great potential as another broadleaved evergreen shrub or tree. It typically can be pruned and shaped into topiary or hedges. It has been used as a street tree in parts of China.

SIZE AND HABIT 30–60 feet (9–18 m) tall, 15–20 feet (5–6 m) wide. Upright, narrow, and columnar densely branched tree or large shrub.
ZONES 8–11
FLOWERS Creamy white with distinctive purple stamens; small and upward facing, with 9–12 tepals. Blooms midspring. Fragrant.
FOLIAGE Evergreen and glossy. New emerging foliage is bronze.
FRUIT Globose reddish pink seedhead is ornamental.
CULTIVATION Full sun to part shade. Propagate by seed or grafting.
ORIGIN Native to Fujian, Guangdong, Guizhou, Hainan, Hunan, Jiangxi, and Zhejiang, China.

Magnolia macrophylla

bigleaf magnolia

This native magnolia has large tropical leaves, much like *Magnolia macrophylla* subsp. *ashei*, *M. fraseri*, and *M. tripetala*. However, the leaves on *M. macrophylla* can be the largest and give the most significant tropical effect in the garden. The fragrant flowers are equally as impressive and even the large fruits can be ornamental in late summer to early autumn. It has been used to great effect on the High Line in New York City. It blooms in late spring to midsummer, or as early as midspring in hotter climates.

SIZE AND HABIT 30–50 feet (9–15 m) tall and wide. Broad, openly branched tree.
ZONES 5–8
FLOWERS Large and cup shaped; 12–18 inches (30–46 cm) across and 3–5 inches (8–13 cm) tall, with 9 tepals. Inner 3 tepals have a purple blotch at the base. Blooms late spring. Fragrant.
FOLIAGE Oblong to spatulate. The leaves are silvery grey beneath and are somewhat undulating.
FRUIT Attractive, cone shaped, and very pubescent; can turn pink to reddish orange at maturity.
CULTIVATION In the wild it grows in moist and shady areas, and while it can grow in these conditions in the garden, it is not limited to them. It can be grown in full sun with a soil rich in organic matter. Propagate by seed.
ORIGIN Native to Ohio and Kentucky south to Georgia and west to Arkansas and Louisiana.

Magnolia macrophylla subsp. *ashei*

Ashe magnolia

Ashe magnolia is very similar in many respects to bigleaf magnolia, *Magnolia macrophylla*, except diminutive in all respects to size, foliage, and flowers. It is also used on the High Line in New York City. For the relatively small garden, it is a wonderful plant for providing a tropical effect. The state champion tree in Torreya State Park is 53 feet (16 m) tall. It is endemic to eight counties in the Florida Panhandle.

SIZE AND HABIT 10–20 feet (3–6 m) tall, 10–15 feet (3–5 m) wide. Small, stout, compact tree or bushy shrub.
ZONES 6–9
FLOWERS Open faced, 12 inches (30 cm) across, with a purple splotch at base of each of the 6 tepals. Blooms late spring. Fragrant.
FOLIAGE With a somewhat wavy or undulating surface.
FRUIT Attractive, cone shaped, and pubescent; turning bright pink to orange-red in late summer to early autumn.
CULTIVATION It can grow in moist woodland situations, but can also grow in full sun with a moisture-retentive soil high in organic matter. Propagate by seed or cuttings.
ORIGIN Native to the Florida Panhandle.

Magnolia 'March Til Frost'

'March Til Frost' is considered a member of the so-called red magnolias as a result of the wine red color of its outer tepals. It has several bursts of flowers throughout the growing season, hence the cultivar name. It typically starts blooming midspring, or as early as late winter in northern Florida (Zone 8).

SIZE AND HABIT 20 feet (6 m) tall, 18 feet (5 m) wide. Upright; small tree to large shrub.
ZONES 5–9
FLOWERS Upright and goblet shaped; 5–8 inch (13–20 cm) across, with deep wine red outer tepals and rose-white inner tepals, making for a striking contrast. Blooms midspring to midsummer.
FOLIAGE Obovate.
CULTIVATION Full sun to part shade. Propagate by cuttings or grafting.
ORIGIN *Magnolia* 'Ruby' × (*M. liliiflora* × *M. cylindrica*), bred by August Kehr.

Magnolia 'Marillyn'

A very hardy cultivar, 'Marillyn' can be in bloom for up to four weeks. A good magnolia for the small garden. It has characteristics similar to The Girls magnolias and shares one of the same parents, *Magnolia liliiflora* 'Nigra'—'Marillyn', however, has a more open habit and is slightly hardier.

SIZE AND HABIT 10–15 feet (3–5 m) tall, 8–12 feet (2–4 m) wide. Large, multi-stemmed shrub.
ZONES 4a–8b
FLOWERS Tulip shaped, with 6 tepals that are wine-red on the outside and flushed white on the inside. Inner tepals have deep pink streaking. Blooms midspring. Slight fragrance.
FOLIAGE Elliptic; new foliage is coppery green.
CULTIVATION Full sun with well-drained soil. Propagate by cuttings or grafting.
ORIGIN *Magnolia liliiflora* 'Nigra' × *M. kobus*, bred by Eva Maria Sperber.

Magnolia officinalis var. *biloba* 'Fireworks'

An exciting new color form for *Magnolia officinalis* var. *biloba*, this very new cultivar first bloomed on 20 May 2013. The large and bold foliage makes it a good choice for a magnolia with a tropical effect and it can be used in ways similar to *M. macrophylla*, *M. macrophylla* subsp. *ashei*, and *M. tripetala*, among others. This was purchased as *M. officinalis* var. *biloba*, but developed pinkish-red flowers.

SIZE AND HABIT 60–70 feet (18–21 m) tall, 30 feet (9 m) wide. Tall, upright tree with a stout and somewhat gawky appearance.

ZONES 6–9

FLOWERS Made up of 2 whorls of 6 tepals each. Each tepal is 6 inches (15 cm) long and 2.5 inches (6 cm) wide. The tepals are dark reddish pink grading to white at the base. Blooms late spring. Strong fragrance.

FOLIAGE Elliptic; green above and grey-green below.

FRUIT Attractive and large, with bright red seeds; will turn red in time.

CULTIVATION Full sun to part shade with well-drained soil; some protection from the wind will preserve the foliage and flowers. Propagate by grafting.

ORIGIN Selected by John Kuhlman.

Magnolia 'Paul Cook'

This fast-growing tree has large spring flowers that are lavendar on the outside and white inside. The combination of *Magnolia* ×*soulangeana* 'Lennei' and *M. sprengeri* var. *diva* 'Diva' has resulted in one of the largest and most ornamental of all magnolias.

SIZE AND HABIT 15–25 feet (5–8 m) tall, 15 feet (5 m) wide. Fast growing and pyramidal; small to medium tree. Upright and more robust than either of its parents.
ZONES 6–9
FLOWERS Large, blousy, and lavender-pink; 8–10 inches (20–25 cm) across, with 6–9 tepals that are white on the inside. Blooms early spring.
FOLIAGE Broadly elliptic.
CULTIVATION Full sun with well-drained soil. Propagate by cuttings or grafting.
ORIGIN *Magnolia* ×*soulangeana* 'Lennei' × *M. sprengeri* var. *diva* 'Diva', bred by Frank Gaylon.

Magnolia 'Pegasus'

This is a very floriferous cultivar and the flowers have good resistance to frost. An Award of Garden Merit winner in 2012.

SIZE AND HABIT 15–30 feet (5–9 m) tall and wide. Upright to arching habit ultimately developing a broad crown.
ZONES 5–9
FLOWERS Upright and pure white with a slight pink cast at base; 4–8 inches (10–20 cm) across, with 9 tepals. Flower shape is similar to those of *M. denudata*, but more slender. Blooms early spring.
FOLIAGE Elliptic.
FRUIT Attractive; bright red and cylindrical.
CULTIVATION Dappled shade with moist soil. Propagate by cuttings or grafting.
ORIGIN *Magnolia cylindrica* × *M. denudata*, bred by Trengwainton Gardens.

Magnolia 'Purple Prince'

Nearly a true purple magnolia, 'Purple Prince' blooms along with the saucer magnolias.

SIZE AND HABIT 15–20 feet (5–6 m) tall and wide. Upright to pyramidal.

ZONES 5–8

FLOWERS The long slender buds open into a cup-and-saucer shape; 10 inches (25 cm) across. There are 9 tepals, 5 inches (13 cm) long, dark purple on the outside and slightly lighter inside. Blooms midspring.

FOLIAGE Obovate.

CULTIVATION Full sun to part shade. Propagate by cuttings or grafting.

ORIGIN *Magnolia liliiflora* 'Darkest Purple' × *M. ×soulangeana* 'Lennei', bred by Frank Gaylon.

Magnolia 'Red Baron'

'Red Baron' has flowers similar to those of 'Big Dude', but smaller and with a deeper red color. A good plant for the extremes of the midwestern states because of its hardiness. The hardiness has been an important component in Dennis Ledvina's breeding program. It blooms at about the same time as 'Daybreak'.

SIZE AND HABIT After 20 years, 40 feet (12 m) tall, 20 feet (6 m) wide. Upright.
ZONES 4–8
FLOWERS Large, deep rose-red, and goblet shaped, with white interiors. Blooms midspring. Mild fragrance.
FOLIAGE Broadly ovate
CULTIVATION Sun to part shade with moist but well-drained soils and protection from the wind. Propagate by cuttings or grafting.
ORIGIN *Magnolia acuminata* × M. 'Big Dude', bred by Dennis Ledvina.

Magnolia 'Rose Marie'

This late-blooming cultivar rarely gets frosted because of the time of flowering. It flowers in midspring, and in late spring in Zone 5. A relatively fast-growing magnolia.

SIZE AND HABIT 18–20 feet (5–6 m) tall, 8–10 feet (2–3 m) wide. Pyramidal and columnar with a small stature.

ZONES 5–8

FLOWERS Upright and broad, landing somewhere between goblet and tulip shaped, with 9 broad tepals. The flowers could also be described as cup-and-saucer in form. The exterior of the tepals are rosy pink and the interiors are medium pink (a shade darker than those of 'Daybreak', one of its parents). It blooms at a young age and is very floriferous; bloom time can last up to six weeks. Flowers appear in midspring as the foliage is emerging. As the flower matures it opens up, exposing the inner color of the tepal. Lemon fragrance.

FOLIAGE Deep green and broadly ovate.

CULTIVATION Sun to part shade with moist but well-drained soils and protection from the wind. Propagate by cuttings or grafting.

ORIGIN *Magnolia* 'Pink Surprise' × *M.* 'Daybreak', bred by Dennis Ledvina.

Magnolia salicifolia

anise magnolia

There was a fantastic specimen of anise magnolia at Scott Arboretum that at maturity had beautiful smooth, grey bark. At Swarthmore (Zone 7), it is one of the earliest magnolias to flower so it always runs the risk of being frosted. It is a parent of the highly ornamental *Magnolia ×kewensis* 'Wada's Memory'.

SIZE AND HABIT 30–50 feet (9–15 m) tall and wide. Broadly pyramidal with age. In youth it is more narrow and upright than broad.

ZONES 4–7

FLOWERS White, 3–6 inches (8–15 cm) across, with 6 tepals. The tepals are 2–4 inches (5–10 cm) long and can have a slight pink color at the base. Blooms early spring. Fragrant; the stems and leaves when scratched also have a lemony or anise fragrance.

FOLIAGE Narrow and oval; reasonable yellow autumn color.

FRUIT Rose-pink.

CULTIVATION Full sun with well-drained soil. Propagate by seed or cuttings.

ORIGIN Native to Honshu, Kyushu, and Shikoku Islands, Japan.

Magnolia ×soulangeana

saucer magnolia
SYNONYM *M. ×soulangeana* 'Etienne
Soulange-Bodin'

The first saucer magnolia flowered in France in 1826, and it has been a classic ever since. At Swarthmore, this is the quintessential flowering tree. There is no other tree that can match the profusion of flowers. They are, however, vulnerable to spring frosts, because they are among the first magnolias to flower in midspring, but most of the damage tends to be superficial and does not actually harm the tree. The two parents play important roles in this hybrid: *Magnolia denudata* brings size, habit, and white and fragrant flowers, while *M. liliiflora* brings purple color and a more compact and rounded habit. An Award of Garden Merit winner in 1993.

SIZE AND HABIT 40 feet (12 m) tall, 45 feet (14 m) wide. Upright when young, becoming a large, multi-trunked magnolia with attractive smooth grey bark over time. At maturity it is a broad canopy, often with wide-reaching branches low to the ground.

ZONES 4–9

FLOWERS Depending on the cultivar, flowers can be white, pink, purple, reddish purple, or even bicolored if the inner tepal is white and the outer tepal has a strong contrasting color; up to 10 inches (25 cm) across, with 9 large, fleshy tepals. Large, silky buds, 0.75 inches (2 cm) long, swell in late winter and add ornamental interest. A true cup-and-saucer magnolia. Blooms early spring. Fragrant.

FOLIAGE Obovate. Like many other magnolias, autumn color can be a golden brown.

CULTIVATION Full sun with well-drained soil. Propagate by cuttings or grafting.

ORIGIN *Magnolia denudata* × *M. liliiflora*, bred by Étienne Soulange-Bodin.

Magnolia ×soulangeana 'Alexandrina'

An old cultivar, selected in 1831, there are apparently a few selections that parade under this name. The one described here is most common in the United States and a clone with white flowers tinged with purple is more common in England.

SIZE AND HABIT 20–30 feet (6–9 m) tall and wide. Upright, oval tree when young, becoming more broadly rounded with time.
ZONES 5–9
FLOWERS Deep red and tulip shaped; 4 inches (10 cm) long, with 9 tepals. Outer tepal is reddish purple and inner tepal is pure white, creating a bicolor effect. Blooms midspring. Fragrant.
FOLIAGE Oblong.
CULTIVATION Full sun with well-drained soil. Propagate by cuttings or grafting.
ORIGIN *Magnolia denudata* × *M. liliiflora*, selected by Cels of Montrouge.

Magnolia ×soulangeana 'Big Pink'

SYNONYM *M. ×soulangeana* Alexandrina Japanese Form

'Big Pink' blooms later than many *Magnolia ×soulangeana* cultivars, thus making it a good choice for colder, wetter climates.

SIZE AND HABIT 30 feet (9 m) tall, 20 feet (6 m) wide. Upright and vase shaped when young, becoming more upright than broad at maturity.
ZONES 5–9
FLOWERS Upright and chalice shaped; lighter pink at the tip of the tepals, and deeper pink toward the base; 4–8 inches (10–20 cm) across. A very floriferous cultivar. Blooms early spring. Fragrant.
FOLIAGE Obovate.
CULTIVATION Full sun with well-drained soil. Propagate by cuttings or grafting.
ORIGIN Bred by K. Sawada.

Magnolia ×soulangeana 'Brozzonii'

A great selection for cold climates both due to its late flowering and its hardiness. It is one of the last to flower of all the *Magnolia ×soulangeana* cultivars. An Award of Garden Merit winner in 1993.

SIZE AND HABIT 25–30 feet (8–9 m) tall and wide. Upright, rounded tree.

ZONES 4–8

FLOWERS Upright and cup-and-saucer shaped; 10 inches (25 cm) across when fully open, with 6 white tepals, 4 inches (10 cm) long; rose-colored veins at the base of inner tepals. Blooms midspring; one of the last to flower of all the *M. ×soulangeana* cultivars. Fragrant.

FOLIAGE Obovate.

CULTIVATION Full sun with well-drained soil. Propagate by cuttings or grafting.

ORIGIN *Magnolia denudata × M. liliiflora,* named in honor of Camillo Brozzoni in 1873.

Magnolia ×soulangeana 'Lennei'

A classic saucer cultivar, with large goblet-shaped, bicolored flowers. It is a small tree, smaller than many of the *Magnolia ×soulangeana* cultivars.

SIZE AND HABIT 15–20 feet (5–6 m) wide and tall. Broadly rounded habit.

ZONES 6–9

FLOWERS Tulip shaped, with broadly ovate tepals, 4 inches (10 cm) long and wide. Tepals are rose-pink on the outside and white on the interior, creating an interesting bicolored effect. Blooms early spring. Fragrant.

FOLIAGE Larger, broader leaves.

CULTIVATION Full sun with well-drained soil. Propagate by cuttings or grafting.

ORIGIN *Magnolia denudata* × *M. liliiflora*, bred by Giuseppe Manetti.

Magnolia ×soulangeana 'Lennei Alba'

A truly pure white magnolia. It flowers profusely in early spring.

SIZE AND HABIT 19 feet (6 m) tall, 13 feet (4 m) wide. Spreading; upright when young.
ZONES 6–9
FLOWERS Large, white, rounded, and goblet shaped, with 9 tepals. Blooms early spring. Fragrant.
FOLIAGE Obovate.
CULTIVATION Full sun with well-drained soil. Propagate by cuttings or grafting.
ORIGIN *Magnolia ×soulangeana* 'Lennei' × *M. denudata*, bred by Karl Otto Froebelin 1905.

Magnolia ×soulangeana 'Lilliputian'

This is the smallest of all the *Magnolia ×soulangeana* cultivars and thus the best saucer magnolia for small gardens and courtyard plantings.

SIZE AND HABIT 12 feet (4 m) tall, 8 feet (2 m) wide. Upright, pyramidal tree, becoming more broad spreading with age.

ZONES 5–9

FLOWERS Pink with pink streaking on the tepals, becoming darker pink toward the base. Blooms early spring. Fragrant.

FOLIAGE Elliptic.

CULTIVATION Full sun with well-drained soil. Propagate by cuttings or grafting.

ORIGIN *Magnolia denudata × M. liliiflora*, bred by Semmes Nursery.

Magnolia ×soulangeana 'Picture'

SYNONYM M. ×*soulangeana* 'Wada's Picture'

This nicely rounded tree has large bicolored flowers that make for a stunning "picture."

SIZE AND HABIT 20–25 feet (6–8 m) tall, 15–25 feet (5–8 m) wide. Distinctly upright in youth, becoming oval and then rounded.

ZONES 5–9

FLOWERS White to pale pink with a deep reddish stain on the middle of the tepal and at the outer base; up to 14 inches (36 cm) across, with tepals up to 7 inches (18 cm) long. Upright and tulip shaped. Blooms early spring. Fragrant.

FOLIAGE Obovate.

CULTIVATION Full sun with well-drained soil. Propagate by cuttings or grafting.

ORIGIN *Magnolia denudata* × *M. liliiflora*, bred by K. Wada.

Magnolia 'Spectrum'

A sister seedling of *Magnolia* 'Galaxy', but the habit is more broadly spreading and the flowers are more sporadically borne. An Award of Garden Merit winner in 2012.

SIZE AND HABIT 25 feet (8 m) tall and wide. Upright, oval to rounded, multi-stemmed tree, becoming broadly pyramidal with age.

ZONES 6–9

FLOWERS Large, 10–12 inches (25–30 cm) across; borne upright and splaying out as the flower matures. With 8–12 deep reddish purple tepals, 5.5 inches (14 cm) long. Inner tepals are pinkish white, with pink striations are on inner and outer tepals. Blooms midspring.

FOLIAGE Elliptic.

CULTIVATION Full sun with well-drained soil. Propagate by cuttings or grafting.

ORIGIN *Magnolia liliiflora* 'Nigra' × *M. sprengeri* var. *diva* 'Diva', bred by William Kosar.

Magnolia sprengeri var. *diva* 'Diva'

Sprenger's magnolia

A hardy selection, and considered one of the most beautiful of all the magnolias. It flowers late enough to escape most frosts.

SIZE AND HABIT 50 feet (15 m) tall, 30 feet (9 m) wide. Upright with an overall oval habit.

ZONES 5b–8

FLOWERS Saucer shaped; 6–8 inches (15–20 cm) across. Tepals, curved in at the tip, are deep rose-pink on the outside and pale pink and streaked on the inside. It produces flowers profusely at young age. Blooms early spring. Strong fragrance.

FOLIAGE Obovate, with silvery pubescence on underside.

CULTIVATION Full sun with well-drained soil. Propagate by cuttings or grafting.

ORIGIN Introduced by E. H. Wilson in 1901.

Magnolia 'Star Wars'

For most parts of the country where *Magnolia campbellii* won't thrive, 'Star Wars' is a good alternative. It blooms for up to six weeks in midspring. An Award of Garden Merit winner in 2002.

SIZE AND HABIT 15 feet (5 m) tall, 20 feet (6 m) wide. Broadly pyramidal at maturity.
ZONES 6b–9
FLOWERS Loosely borne and soft pink; 11 inches (28 m) across, with 12 tepals that splay out as the flower matures, giving it a look similar to its relative, *M. campbellii*. Tepals have a deeper pink flush at the base and are lighter on inside. Blooms early spring. Fragrant.
FOLIAGE Ovate, large, and glossy green, with a tapering tip.
CULTIVATION Full sun to part shade with well-drained soil. Propagate by cuttings or grafting.
ORIGIN *Magnolia campbellii* × *M. liliiflora*, bred by Oswald Blumhardt.

Magnolia stellata
star magnolia

As one of the earliest of the spring-flowering magnolias, *Magnolia stellata* is a true harbinger of spring. The dense branches makes the display of flowers on the leafless branches in spring especially impressive. Some cultivars can have from 12–40 tepals. The flowers can be white, light pink, and even darker pink, and flowering starts when the plants are quite young, only one or two years old. It is one of the hardiest of all the magnolias.

SIZE AND HABIT 20 feet (6 m) tall and wide. Large, multi-stemmed shrub or small tree depending on how it is trained and pruned when young.

ZONES 4–9

FLOWERS Relatively small and white; 4 inches (10 cm) across, with 12–18 tepals, 2 inches (5 cm) long. Very showy as a result of the many tepals. Blooms early spring. Fragrant.

FOLIAGE Elliptic.

CULTIVATION Full sun with well-drained soil. Because it blooms so early, avoid planting in southern exposures (in the Northern Hemisphere), which can cause the buds to flower prematurely and make them more vulnerable to getting frosted. Propagate by seed or cuttings.

ORIGIN Native to Japan.

Magnolia stellata 'Centennial'

'Centennial' was introduced by the Arnold Arboretum in 1972 to celebrate its centennial. It is one of the finest medium-sized magnolias for the landscape. It is very popular as a result of its hardiness. It blooms in late winter in climates where the average winter temperature doesn't drop below 15°F (−9°C). An Award of Garden Merit winner in 2012, and a recipient of the Gold Medal from the Pennsylvania Horticultural Society.

SIZE AND HABIT 25 feet (8 m) tall, 22 feet (7 m) wide. Broadly pyramidal at maturity.
ZONES 4–9
FLOWERS Pure white, but occasionally with a touch of pink; 5.5 inches (14 cm) across, with 28–33 tepals, 1.5–2 inches (4–5 cm) long, giving off a doubling effect. Blooms early spring. Fragrant.
FOLIAGE Elliptic; deciduous.
CULTIVATION Full sun with well-drained soil. Propagate by cuttings or grafting.
ORIGIN Seedling of M. stellata 'Rosea', selected by Arnold Arboretum.

Magnolia stellata 'Chrysanthemumiflora'

'Chrysanthemumiflora' is a good choice for small gardens with an incredible profusion of powder pink flowers. One of the most floriferous of all magnolias.

SIZE AND HABIT 10–15 feet (3–5 m) tall, 10 feet (3 m) wide. Large, multi-stemmed shrub or small tree depending on how it is trained and pruned when young.
ZONES 4–9
FLOWERS Pale pink, with up to 40 tepals, giving a doubling effect. Each tepal has a deeper pink streak down the middle. Blooms early spring. Fragrant.
FOLIAGE Elliptic.
CULTIVATION Full sun with well-drained soil. Because it blooms so early, avoid planting in southern exposures (in the Northern Hemisphere), which can cause the buds to flower prematurely and make them more vulnerable to getting frosted. Propagate by cuttings or grafting.
ORIGIN Seedling of M. stellata 'Rubra', bred by K. Wada.

Magnolia stellata 'Encore'

A slow-growing, but very bushy and full cultivar, 'Encore' is a very floriferous plant. Its parentage is not clear since it was an open-pollinated seedling from *Magnolia ×loebneri* 'Ballerina'.

SIZE AND HABIT 15 feet (5 m) tall, 10–15 feet (3–5 m) wide. Large, multi-stemmed shrub or small tree depending on how it is trained and pruned when young.

ZONES 4–8

FLOWERS Pink buds opening to many-tepaled (up to 20–25) white flowers with a boss of golden stamens. The white tepals have a hint of pink in the center and at the base. Buds form in multiples of one to four at the tips of the branches, adding to the floral display. Blooms early spring.

FOLIAGE Elliptic.

CULTIVATION Full sun with well-drained soil. Because it blooms so early, avoid planting in southern exposures (in the Northern Hemisphere), which can cause the buds to flower prematurely and make them more vulnerable to getting frosted. Propagate by cuttings or grafting.

ORIGIN Seedling of *M. ×loebneri* 'Ballerina', bred by August Kehr.

Magnolia stellata 'Royal Star'

'Royal Star' is one of the most common *Magnolia stellata* cultivars. It is more robust and faster growing and blooms seven to ten days earlier. An Award of Garden Merit winner in 2012.

SIZE AND HABIT 15 feet (5 m) tall, 12 feet (4 m) wide. Large, multi-stemmed shrub or small tree depending on how it is trained and pruned when young.
ZONES 4–9
FLOWERS Pink buds opening to large white flowers with a slight touch of pink; up to 6 inches (15 cm) across, with 25–30 tepals. Blooms early spring. Fragrant.
FOLIAGE Elliptic.
CULTIVATION Full sun with well-drained soil. Because it blooms so early, avoid planting in southern exposures (in the Northern Hemisphere), which can cause the buds to flower prematurely and make them more vulnerable to getting frosted. Propagate by cuttings or grafting.
ORIGIN Seedling of *M. stellata* 'Waterlily', selected by John Vermuelen.

Magnolia 'Sweetheart'

A great medium-sized magnolia. An Award of Garden Merit winner in 2012.

SIZE AND HABIT 15 feet (5 m) tall, 9 feet (3 m) wide. Upright.
ZONES 7–9
FLOWERS Upright, cup shaped, and bubble gum pink; with 12 broad tepals that are lighter on the inner tepal. Blooms early spring. Fragrant.
FOLIAGE Obovate.
CULTIVATION Sun to part shade with well-drained soil and protection from the wind. Propagate by cuttings or grafting.
ORIGIN *Magnolia sprengeri* var. *diva* 'Diva' × *M. sargentiana* var. *robusta*, bred by Peter Cave.

Magnolia 'Tina Durio'

A Gresham hybrid with large pure white flowers with thick tepals.

SIZE AND HABIT 25–30 feet (8–9 m) tall and wide. Fast growing.
ZONES 6–10
FLOWERS Very large, goblet shaped, and pure white; 10–12 inches (25–30 cm) across. Open faced, with 9–12 broad tepals with a hint of lighter pink on the outer tepal. Flowers resemble those of *M. campbellii* 'Alba'. Blooms early spring. Fragrant.
FOLIAGE Obovate.
CULTIVATION Sun to part shade with well-drained soil. Propagate by cuttings or grafting.
ORIGIN *Magnolia* ×*veitchii* × *M.* ×*soulangeana* 'Lennei Alba', bred by Todd Gresham.

Magnolia 'Tranquility'

This is another great August Kehr introduction with pale yellow flowers with a rosy blush at the base of the tepals. The open-faced, skyward-facing flowers look similar to those of 'Gold Star' and 'Sunburst' in their arrangement.

SIZE AND HABIT 15 feet (5 m) tall, 20 feet (6 m) wide. Rounded tree.
ZONES 5a–8b
FLOWERS Pale yellow and open faced; 8 inches (20 cm) across. Flowers have a rose blush at the base. Blooms midspring.
FOLIAGE Large and wavy.
CULTIVATION Full sun with well-drained soil. Propagate by cuttings or grafting.
ORIGIN *Magnolia* ×*brooklynensis* 'Woodsman' × *M.* 'Gold Star', bred by August Kehr.

Magnolia tripetala
umbrella tree

The species was discovered in 1743 by Mark Catesby. Of all magnolias grown in cultivation, umbrella tree has the largest leaves. Like other North American native magnolias, such as *Magnolia macrophylla*, *M. macrophylla* subsp. *ashei*, and *M. fraseri*, it has tropical-looking leaves, which makes it effective in spaces where bold texture is needed. At Scott Arboretum it is planted as a backdrop for the fine-foliaged thread-leaf bluestar, *Amsonia hubrictii*. It is also used to great effect on the High Line in New York City.

SIZE AND HABIT 50 feet (15 m) tall, 30 feet (9 m) wide. Upright, coarse habit because of the large leaves. It can be grown as a single- or multi-stemmed specimen.
ZONES 5–9
FLOWERS White; 4–5 inches (10–13 cm) across, with 6–9 tepals. Blooms midspring.
FOLIAGE Very large, up to 24 inches (61 cm) long and 8 inches (20 cm) wide. Dark green above and grey-green below. Deciduous.
FRUIT Conelike; turning from pink to red.
CULTIVATION In the wild, it grows in deep moist woods; in cultivation, it can be grown as an understory tree, but also as a specimen tree in full sun. Propagate by seed.
ORIGIN Native from Pennsylvania to Georgia and west to Mississippi and Arkansas.

Magnolia 'Twiggy'

The form of this small tree would make a perfect specimen for hedging or where an upright, broadleaved evergreen is needed.

SIZE AND HABIT After 13 years, 16 feet (5 m) tall, 12 feet (4 m) wide. Very densely branched, compact, pyramidal tree.
ZONES 7–10
FLOWERS Resembling those of *M. figo* var. *skinneriana*, but white instead of creamy yellow. The edge of the tepals have a pinkish purple blush that is also found at the base of tepals. Flowers are sparsely produced. Blooms midspring, with repeat flowering in summer. Sweet fragrance.
FOLIAGE Small and evergreen.
CULTIVATION Full sun with well-drained soil. Propagate by cuttings.
ORIGIN *Magnolia elegantifolia* × (possibly) *M. figo*, bred by Richard Figlar.

Magnolia virginiana var. *australis*
sweetbay magnolia

There are two varieties of *Magnolia virginiana*: variety *australis*, which is found in the southern states, and the northern form, variety *virginiana*, which is found on the Coastal Plain from North Carolina to Massachusetts. The twigs and pedicels are covered with white silky hairs, which is an identifying characteristic of the southern variety. The southern variety also has a more lemony fragrance. When grown in colder and wetter northern climates, variety *australis* will be evergreen to partially evergreen to deciduous depending on the clone and depending on the severity of winter. There are several dwarf and small-leaved forms, including 'Coosa', 'Perdido', and 'Tensaw', and in some parts of Florida, natural dwarfing will occur. While it is generally a Coastal Plain species, it does grow into the more hilly Piedmont in Tennessee, Georgia, Oklahoma, and Arkansas. When the wind blows the leaves turn, revealing their silvery undersides; this in itself is an ornamental attribute. In the Midwest chlorosis will often occur due to the high pH of soils. Common names also include swamp bay and swamp laurel, probably making reference to the laurellike leaves of the bay, *Laurus nobilis*.

SIZE AND HABIT Up to 90 feet (27 m) tall in the wild, but typically no more than 45–50 feet (14–15 m) tall, 20–30 feet (6–9 m) wide in cultivation. Upright tree with spreading canopy, becoming broadly pyramidal over time.

ZONES 6–10

FLOWERS Creamy white; 2–3 inches (5–8 cm) across, with 9–12 small tepals. Often found sporadically throughout the canopy and not in heavy profusion like many of the spring-flowering magnolias. Blooms late spring, sporadically through summer. Lemon fragrance.

FOLIAGE Ovate and glossy dark green, with silvery undersides. Evergreen leaves drop in spring as buds emerge.

CULTIVATION Full sun to full shade. It will thrive in normal garden soils, but it is one of the few magnolias that can take marshy to wet soils and even standing water, which is often where it is found in natural settings. It requires acid soils, but is also more tolerant of shade than most magnolias. Propagate by seed or grafting.

ORIGIN Native to South Carolina south to Florida and west to Texas. A population also occurs in Cuba.

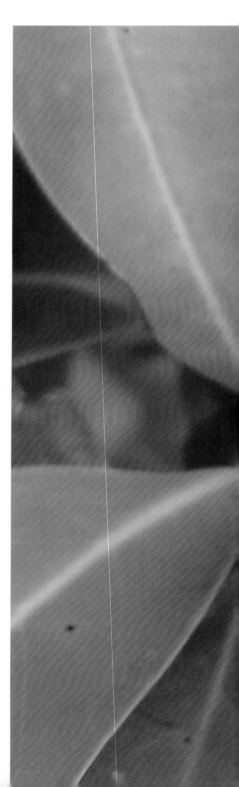

Magnolia virginiana var. *australis* 'Green Shadow'

SYNONYM *M. virginiana* var. *australis* 'Greenbay'

One of the most evergreen cultivars for the cold and wet northern regions. On the High Line in New York City it has proven to be completely evergreen. Promoted by the University of Arkansas Division of Agriculture as an alternative hedge plant. It has suffered considerable leaf damage at −20°F (−29°C) degrees.

SIZE AND HABIT 35 feet (11 m) tall, 18 feet (5 m) wide. Forming a tight oval tree over time. Can be grown as a single- or multi-stemmed tree.

ZONES 5–10

FLOWERS Small and creamy white; 2–3 inches (5–8 cm) across, with 9–12 tepals. Often found sporadically throughout the canopy and not in heavy profusion like many of the spring-flowering magnolias. Blooms late spring. Lemon fragrance.

FOLIAGE Ovate and glossy dark green, with silvery undersides. Evergreen leaves drop in spring as buds emerge. Fully evergreen in Zone 7.

CULTIVATION Full sun to full shade. It will thrive in normal garden soils, but it is one of the few magnolias that can take marshy to wet soils and even standing water, which is often where it is found in natural settings. It requires acid soils, but is also more tolerant of shade than most magnolias. Propagate by grafting.

ORIGIN Selection made by Don Shadow from seedlings obtained from Illinois plantsman J. C. McDaniel.

Magnolia virginiana var. *australis* 'Henry Hicks'

This cultivar was selected at Scott Arboretum by their first director, John Wister, who named it in honor of Long Island nurseryman Henry Hicks. It can be almost completely evergreen in Zone 7, and it makes a nice addition to a native landscape or used as an accent tree in a small to medium-sized garden. Grows natively in the Coastal Plain and is one of the few magnolias that can grow in marshy and poorly drained soils.

SIZE AND HABIT 40 feet (12 m) tall, 30 feet (9 m) wide in cultivation. Upright, with spreading habit over time. Many trees are multi-stemmed, but it can be grown as a single-trunked tree.

ZONES 6b–10

FLOWERS Single and white; to 3 inches (8 cm) across, with 9–12 tepals. Blooms late spring, and sporadically into summer. Lemon fragrance.

FOLIAGE Elliptic to lanceolate; glossy dark green above and pale to glaucous underneath. Semi-evergreen to evergreen.

CULTIVATION Thrives best in full sun. It can be grown as understory plant, but flowering will be reduced. It is one of the very few magnolias that can grow in poorly drained soils, swampy sites, or at the edge of bodies of water. In colder climates, evergreen types may exhibit leaf loss in winter. Propagate by cuttings or grafting.

ORIGIN Selected by John Wister.

Magnolia virginiana var. *australis* 'Mattie Mae Smith'

SYNONYM *M. virginiana* var. *australis* 'Mardi Gras'

A good variegated broadleaved evergreen to lighten a dark spot in the garden. Depending on your location, it can be evergreen, semi-evergreen, or deciduous. In spite of its variegation, it has outstanding vigor. It could be trained as an interesting espalier.

SIZE AND HABIT 15 feet (5 m) tall, 10 feet (3 m) wide. Often a multi-stemmed tree or shrub, but can be grown as a single-stemmed tree.

ZONES 6–10

FLOWERS Creamy white; 2–3 inches (5–8 cm) across, with 9–12 small tepals. Often found sporadically throughout the canopy and not in heavy profusion like many of the spring-flowering magnolias. Blooms late spring, and sporadically into summer. Lemon fragrance.

FOLIAGE Elliptic, with a dark green splotch in the center surrounded by an outer sulfur-yellow border.

CULTIVATION Full sun to full shade. It will thrive in normal garden soils, but it is one of the few magnolias that can take marshy to wet soils and even standing water, which is often where it is found in natural settings. It requires acid soils, but is also more tolerant of shade than most magnolias. Growth will be greater in full sun, though too much too soon can bleach the foliage. Propagate by cuttings or grafting.

ORIGIN Selected by John Allen Smith.

Magnolia virginiana var. *australis* 'Ned's Northern Belle'

Touted as the hardiest cultivar of the southern sweetbay magnolias, 'Ned's Northern Belle' has retained foliage in sub-zero temperatures and survived temperatures as low as −35°F (−37°C). It originated in Ohio (Zone 4), where it blooms in early to midsummer.

SIZE AND HABIT 25 feet (8 m) tall, 8–9 feet (2–3 m) wide. Tall and narrow and nearly fastigiate.
ZONES 3b–10
FLOWERS Creamy white; 2–3 inches (5–8 cm) across, with 9–12 small tepals. Often found sporadically throughout the canopy and not in heavy profusion like many of the spring-flowering magnolias. Blooms late spring, and sporadically into summer. Lemon fragrance.
FOLIAGE Ovate and glossy dark green, with silvery undersides. Evergreen leaves drop in spring as buds emerge.
FRUIT Attractive clusters of shiny red fruits in late summer or early autumn.
CULTIVATION Full sun to full shade. It will thrive in normal garden soils, but it is one of the few magnolias that can take marshy to wet soils and even standing water, which is often where it is found in natural settings. It requires acid soils, but is also more tolerant of shade than most magnolias. Provide protection for younger plants, especially in colder climates. Propagate by cuttings or grafting.
ORIGIN From Coles Nursery, bred by Ned Rader.

Magnolia virginiana var. *australis* 'Satellite'

Selected by Frank Santamour at the US National Arboretum from seed he collected in Tennessee. Good evergreen plant in Zone 6, and reliably evergreen at the Arnold Arboretum in Boston, Massachusetts (Zone 7). At Swarthmore in winter 2014–2015, where temperatures reached –2°F (–19°C), this cultivar remained evergreen throughout winter.

SIZE AND HABIT 20 feet (6 m) tall, 15 feet (5 m) wide. Single-stemmed tree with upright, oval canopy.
ZONES 6–10
FLOWERS Creamy white; 2–3 inches (5–8 cm) across, with 9–12 small tepals. Often found sporadically throughout the canopy and not in heavy profusion like many of the spring-flowering magnolias. Blooms late spring, and sporadically into summer. Lemon fragrance.
FOLIAGE Evergreen as far north as Washington, DC. Ovate and glossy dark green, with silvery undersides. Evergreen leaves drop in spring as buds emerge. Beautiful linear leaves with good glossy surface.
FRUIT Attractive clusters of shiny red fruits in late summer or early autumn.
CULTIVATION Full sun to full shade. It will thrive in normal garden soils, but it is one of the few magnolias that can take marshy to wet soils and even standing water, which is often where it is found in natural settings. It requires acid soils, but is also more tolerant of shade than most magnolias. Propagate by cuttings or grafting.
ORIGIN Selected by Frank Santamour, Jr.

Magnolia virginiana var. australis 'Santa Rosa'

This is the hardiest of the *Magnolia virginiana* cultivars, and at the Scott Arboretum, one of the most striking. It makes a beautiful small tree with a nice round canopy and large glossy leaves.

SIZE AND HABIT 25 feet (8 m) tall, 20 feet (6 m) wide. Upright tree with spreading canopy, over time becoming broadly pyramidal. Can develop a strong central leader with a rounded canopy. Vigorous, growing as much as 3–4 feet (1 m) each year.

ZONES 6–10

FLOWERS Creamy white; 2–3 inches (5–8 cm) across, with 9–12 small tepals. Often found sporadically throughout the canopy and not in heavy profusion like many of the spring-flowering magnolias. Blooms late spring, and sporadically into summer. Lemon fragrance.

FOLIAGE Evergreen; undersides have an attractive silver cast. The leaves are longer and wider than on many cultivars, and more glossy; from a distance can almost look like southern magnolia, *Magnolia grandiflora*.

CULTIVATION Full sun to full shade. It will thrive in normal garden soils, but it one of the few magnolias that can take marshy to wet soils and even standing water, which is often where it is found in natural settings. It requires acid soils, but is also more tolerant of shade than most magnolias. Propagate by cuttings or grafting.

ORIGIN Seedling from Santa Rosa County, Florida, selected by Woodlanders Nursery, Inc.

Magnolia virginiana var. *australis* Sweet Thing 'Perry Paige'

Created by George Dodson of Sleepy Hollow Nursery and Fernando Campbell Boyd III of Boyd Nursery Company. This was discovered among a batch of seedlings where after a few years all the other seedlings were becoming treelike, while Sweet Thing 'Perry Paige' remained compact and shrublike in its habit. It is being promoted as an alternative for hedges made out of holly and other broadleaved evergreen shrubs. It is also promoted as a foundation plant or used in large containers.

SIZE AND HABIT 8 feet (2 m) tall, 6 feet (2 m) wide. Dwarf magnolia grown as a rounded, multi-stemmed shrub, ultimately forming a shrublike tree.

ZONES 6b–10

FLOWERS Creamy white; 2–3 inches (5–8 cm) across, with 9–12 small tepals. Often found sporadically throughout the canopy and not in heavy profusion like many of the spring-flowering magnolias. Over time, flowers open up into more of a flattened saucer shape. Blooms late spring, and sporadically into summer. Lemon fragrance.

FOLIAGE Ovate and evergreen; dark green and lustrous above, with a blue-white cast below. The leaves are longer and more slender than on many cultivars.

FRUIT Attractive clusters of shiny red fruit in late summer or early autumn.

CULTIVATION Full sun to full shade. It will thrive in normal garden soils, but it one of the few magnolias that can take marshy to wet soils and even standing water, which is often where it is found in natural settings. It requires acid soils, but is also more tolerant of shade than most magnolias. Propagate by cuttings or grafting.

ORIGIN Selected by George Dodson and Fernando Campbell Boyd III.

Magnolia virginiana var. *virginiana*

sweetbay magnolia

Not even 50 miles east of Swarthmore, the Piedmont quickly changes to the Coastal Plain as does the flora. In these lowland areas where the soil is sandy, you will begin to find *Magnolia virginiana* var. *virginiana* growing in marshy areas along with *Clethra alnifolia* and *Ilex glabra*. It is typically an understory tree growing among *Nyssa sylvatica* and *Acer rubrum*. On a birding trip not too long ago, it was found growing on the edge of a lake with most of its roots completely submerged. In the wet woods of New York it is often associated with the sweetgum, *Liquidambar styraciflua*. The northern form of the sweetbay magnolia, it is characterized as being more deciduous and tends to have multiple stems and provides a thicketlike aspect in the landscape. Almost all the cultivars on the market are variety *australis* selections. It is sometimes referred to as beaver bay because of the tendency of beavers to eat the roots. Early settlers supposedly baited beaver traps with sweetbay magnolia roots.

SIZE AND HABIT 30 feet (9 m) tall; the spread is somewhat unlimited since it grows into a thicket over time. Upright, multi-stemmed, becoming shrub- or thicketlike over time.
ZONES 5–9
FLOWERS Creamy white; 2–3 inches (5–8 cm) across, with 9–12 small tepals. Often found sporadically throughout the canopy and not in heavy profusion like many of the spring-flowering magnolias. Blooms late spring, and sporadically into summer. Lemon fragrance.
FOLIAGE Elliptic, with silvery white undersides. Deciduous.
FRUIT Attractive clusters of shiny red fruits in late summer or early autumn.
CULTIVATION Full sun to full shade. It will thrive in normal garden soils, but it is one of the few magnolias that can take marshy to wet soils and even standing water, which is often where it is found in natural settings. It requires acid soils, but is also more tolerant of shade than most magnolias. Propagate by seed or cuttings.
ORIGIN Native to North Carolina to Massachusetts along the Coastal Plain.

Magnolia 'Vulcan'

'Vulcan' was introduced by Mark Jury in 1990. A sister to 'Apollo', it is smaller than some of the other Jury cultivars such as 'Athene', 'Atlas', 'Lotus', and 'Milky Way'. This cultivar could be categorized as one of the red-flowering magnolias, although the color is more of a purple-red than a true red. This relatively small magnolia is a good selection for gardens with limited space. Because of its narrow habit, especially when young it makes a perfect magnolia for tight quarters. While it flowers at a young age, the flowers tend to be more pink than red, but as the tree matures they will have more of a reddish coloration. The large silky (hairy) buds in winter are also attractive. In some parts of the world, it can flower too early and run the risk of being frosted.

SIZE AND HABIT 15 feet (5 m) tall, 10 feet (3 m) wide in ten years. Upright, single-, or multi-trunked small tree with an oval habit, becoming more rounded with age.
ZONES 6–9
FLOWERS Large, ruby-red, and similar to those of *M. campbellii*; cup-and-saucer shaped, up to 10–12 inches (25–30 cm) across. The 12 slightly curled tepals have a faint blush of white in the center. Blooms early spring. Fragrant.
FOLIAGE Large and obovate.
CULTIVATION Full sun with well-drained soil. Propagate by cuttings or grafting.
ORIGIN *Magnolia campbellii* subsp. *mollicomata* 'Lanarth' × *M. liliiflora* hybrid, bred by Felix Jury.

Magnolia ×wieseneri

Wiesner magnolia
SYNONYM *Magnolia ×watsonii*

Most likely a spontaneous hybrid from a Japanese garden. 'Aashild Kalleberg' is a very floriferous cultivar with 8–9 pure white sepals and a boss of purple-red stamens.

SIZE AND HABIT 20 feet (6 m) tall and wide. Multi-stemmed broad shrub to spreading small tree. Can have a big or a rangy habit.

ZONES 6–9

FLOWERS Tea cup shaped and upward facing; 4–5 inches (10–13 cm) across, with 9 white tepals and a boss of red stamens. After a few days, flowers splay open to 6–8 inches (15–20 cm) and become less attractive. Blooms late spring, and sporadically into summer. Delicious spicy and aromatic fragrance that resembles pineapple.

FOLIAGE Obovate and leathery.

CULTIVATION Full sun with well-drained soil. Propagate by grafting.

ORIGIN *Magnolia obovata* × *M. sieboldii* subsp. *japonica*.

Magnolia wilsonii
Wilson's magnolia

Named for E. H. Wilson, who discovered it in 1904, Wilson's magnolia is an interesting flowering shrub, but not as attractive as *Magnolia sieboldii*. It is characterized by brown to black stems, which can add interest in winter. An Award of Garden Merit winner in 1993.

SIZE AND HABIT 20 feet (6 m) tall and wide. Broad-spreading small tree or large shrub with multiple stems. It can look a little rangy.

ZONES 6–8

FLOWERS White and slightly cup shaped; 4 inches (10 cm) across, with 9 tepals and a boss of attractive purple stamens. Can be similar to those of *M. sieboldii* and pendant, but they can also be more outward facing. Plants will start flowering at five to seven years. Blooms late spring. Fragrant.

FOLIAGE Elliptic. The undersides of the leaves are light brown with hairs that ultimately turn silvery.

FRUIT Pinkish fruiting cones appearing in autumn.

CULTIVATION Grows as an understory shrub in dense woodlands in the wild, and while it can grow that way in cultivation, it will flower better in part sun with a moisture-retentive soil. Propagate by seed.

ORIGIN Native to Gansu, Sichuan, Yunnan, and Guizhou, China.

Magnolia 'Wim Rutten'

Wim Rutten is a Dutch magnolia lover and the founder of magnoliastore.com, and this cultivar is named after him. The form of the tree would make for a good upright street tree.

SIZE AND HABIT 25 feet (8 m) tall, 12 feet (4 m) wide. Upright, oval to pyramidal tree.
ZONES 7–8
FLOWERS 7.5 inches (19 cm) across when fully open. Tepals are a reddish purple, contrasting nicely with the boss of red stamens. Insides and edges of tepals are white, creating a somewhat bicolored effect. Blooms early spring and sometimes sporadically into late spring. Papaya fragrance.
FOLIAGE Obovate.
CULTIVATION Full sun with well-drained soil. Propagate by cuttings.
ORIGIN *Magnolia denudata* 'Forrest's Pink' × *M*. 'Marillyn', bred by Philippe de Spoelberch.

Magnolia 'Yellow Bird'

One of several great magnolias to came out of Brooklyn Botanic Garden's breeding program at Kitchawan Research Station in Ossining, New York. This is one of the best yellow magnolias for the temperate climate of the Pacific Northwest. Flowers emerge at the same time as the foliage. It blooms later than the popular *Magnolia* 'Elizabeth', and blooms for up to three weeks.

SIZE AND HABIT 40 feet (12 m) tall, 30 feet (9 m) wide. Pyramidal, fast growing.
ZONES 5–6
FLOWERS The compact, lemon-yellow, cup-shaped flowers are held upright with a slight greenish tinge to the outer tepals. The 6 tepals are up to 3.5 inches (9 cm) long and 2 inches (5 cm) wide. Blooms late spring.
FOLIAGE Elliptic.
CULTIVATION Full sun with well-drained soil. Propagate by cuttings or grafting.
ORIGIN *Magnolia* ×*brooklynensis* 'Eva Maria' × *M. acuminata* var. *subcordata*, bred by Doris Stone.

Magnolia 'Yellow Lantern'

'Yellow Lantern' is a great hardy magnolia for the extremes of the Midwest and has a somewhat smaller habit than many of the yellow magnolias. An Award of Garden Merit winner in 2012.

SIZE AND HABIT 20 feet (6 m) tall, 15 feet (5 m) wide. Upright, symmetrical tree with strong central leader and oval canopy. Fastigiate, small to medium tree with fairly compact habit.
ZONES 5–8
FLOWERS Lemon yellow and tulip shaped; 6–8 inches (15–20 cm) across, with a slight pinkish coloring in the midrib of the tepal and especially at the base. Blooms late spring. Fragrant.
FOLIAGE Elliptic.
CULTIVATION Full sun with well-drained soil. Propagate by cuttings or grafting.
ORIGIN *Magnolia acuminata* var. *subcordata* 'Miss Honeybee' × *M.* ×*soulangeana* 'Alexandrina', bred by Phil Savage.

Magnolia yuyuanensis

Chinese wood-lotus

SYNONYM *Manglietia yuyuanensis*

This new broadleaved evergreen has great potential for hedging and screening in the garden. In regions where winter temperatures drop below 0°F (−18°C), it would benefit from protection like planting in a courtyard. It grows quite large in its native habitats, but in cultivation will probably be much smaller. It is a montane forest species in the wild. It bloomed heavily at Camellia Forest Nursery in North Carolina (Zone 7b).

SIZE AND HABIT 30 feet (9 m) tall, 15 feet (5 m) wide in cultivation, but up to 60–80 feet (18–24 m) tall, 30–50 feet (9–15 m) wide in the wild. Dense, upright, pyramidal small tree to large shrub.

ZONES 7a–10

FLOWERS Pure white, upward facing, and cup shaped; 4–5 inches (10–13 cm) across, with a boss of red stamens. The outermost tepals can have a plum pink cast. Flowering only lasts for 36 hours, but can occur over a long period of time. Blooms late spring and throughout summer.

FOLIAGE Narrow, glossy, evergreen, and boatlike.

FRUIT Pinkish red, bulbous, and somewhat attractive.

CULTIVATION Sun to part shade with well-drained soil. Propagate by seed or cuttings.

ORIGIN Native to Yunnan, Sichuan, and Guizhou, China.

Magnolia zenii
Zen's magnolia

A good tree for small spaces. Because of the precocious nature of the flowering, Zen's magnolias are often damaged by late frosts. Rare and endemic in the wild. On the West Coast (Zone 8), it can bloom as early as late winter. 'Pink Parchment' is a pink cultivar, but probably of hybrid origin.

SIZE AND HABIT 16–23 feet (5–7 m) tall, 12 feet (4 m) wide. Upright small tree or large shrub with multiple stems.
ZONES 5b–9
FLOWERS Upward facing and tulip shaped; 5 inches (13 cm) across, with 9 white tepals, 3 inches (8 cm) long and flushed pink in the veins and at the base. The abundance of buds covered in silky hairs provides reasonable winter interest. Blooms early spring. Strong fragrance.
FOLIAGE Oblong.
FRUIT Scarlet colored.
CULTIVATION Full sun to part shade. Propagate by seed or cuttings.
ORIGIN Native to Jiangsu, China.

GROWING
AND
PROPAGATING

D

There are many climates throughout the world that are conducive to growing magnolias, which makes magnolias a great option for gardeners (almost) everywhere. In fact, only in areas with extremely cold temperatures or those with desert conditions will you face any significant difficulty. The climate in the southwest of England and parts of New Zealand is excellent for growing *Magnolia campbellii*, *M. sprengeri* var. *sprengeri*, and *M. sargentiana*, while San Francisco is one of the few places in North America where *M. campbellii* can be grown, along with *M. doltsopa* and *M. dawsoniana*. Many parts of California, the Pacific Northwest, and the southeastern United States, as well as warmer areas of Europe, Australia, and New Zealand, would be well suited to growing many of the new evergreen Asian species, such as *M. lotungensis*, *M. maudiae*, *M. insignis*, and *M. foveolata*. There are several cold-hardy species, such as *M. denudata*, *M. stellata*, *M. kobus*, and *M. acuminata*, that do very well in the midwestern and far western United States and would thrive in northern Europe. The Flink Arboretum in southern Sweden can grow over 400 taxa of magnolias.

Hardiness

As shown throughout this book, there are indeed magnolias that can grow in very cold parts of the world. In Minnesota, several spring-flowering magnolias are considered fine ornamentals, such as *Magnolia ×loebneri* 'Leonard Messel', The Girls ('Jane' and 'Susan'), and several star magnolia (*M. stellata*) cultivars. Conversely, there are many

magnolias that will grow in hotter areas like southern Florida, Texas, California, southern Europe, Australia, and northern New Zealand.

In areas where spring comes early or winters can be mild there is always the chance that some magnolias will flower early. These magnolias are most vulnerable to cold temperatures caused by freezing and frosts. Early-flowering species like *M. campbellii*, *M. kobus*, *M. salicifolia*, and *M. denudata* are most susceptible. Often a frost might cause superficial damage to the petals, but if cold temperatures occur when the plant is actively growing (pushing new growth) then there could be significant stem damage and possibly even death to the magnolia. In the United Kingdom, for example, *M. macrophylla* continues growing late into autumn and runs the risk of being damaged by early autumn cold temperatures.

There are many parts of the world where cold-hardy magnolias are important. In the United States, most areas of the Midwest and far West rely on these species and cultivars to contribute to their floral show in the spring. The Magnolia Society International has members growing ornamental magnolias in Ukraine, Estonia, and Russia, and the annual meeting in 2015 is in Poland. Magnolias in this category would be hardy in Zones 4–6.

While cold temperatures can impact magnolias, the amount of exposure to warm temperatures can also have an effect. Magnolias need sufficient summer temperatures to ensure good ripening of growth; if this does not occur, dieback and, in some cases, even death could occur over winter. The amount of exposure to heat can also impact flower color. In areas like Georgia and northern Florida, extreme heat and intense sunlight can contribute to giving many yellow magnolias a more washed out or pale color. Many of the Gresham hybrids will have a more saturated flower color in New York, but in the United Kingdom, where temperatures are generally cooler, the red-purple colors tend to be pink.

Cold-Hardy Magnolias

The Girls series
Magnolia acuminata
Magnolia 'Coral Lake'
Magnolia 'Daybreak'
Magnolia denudata
Magnolia 'Galaxy'
Magnolia 'Judy Zuk'
Magnolia ×*kewensis* 'Wada's Memory'
Magnolia macrophylla
Magnolia sieboldii
Magnolia ×*soulangeana* and cultivars
Magnolia stellata 'Centennial'
Magnolia 'Yellow Lantern'

Exposure

While magnolias in their natural habits would typically be understory plants growing in some amount of shade, and while they can indeed thrive in shade, best flowering for most plants will occur in sunny locations. However, in areas where summers are hot and dry, providing magnolias "high" or dappled shade would be beneficial. Some species, such as *Magnolia macrophylla*, *M. fraseri*, *M. fraseri* var. *pyramidata*, *M. wilsonii*, and *M. sieboldii*, will even do better in partial shade. These would be good options for woodland gardens.

It is also important to make sure that magnolias are not allowed to dry out during summer months. The root systems on magnolias are shallow and therefore mulching around the tree in a planting bed or as a specimen tree in the lawn would be advantageous. At Scott Arboretum, magnolias were mulched every spring with a mixture of

50 percent leaf compost and 50 percent partially decomposed wood chips. Mulching the trees helps suppress weeds, adds organic matter to the soil, and helps retain moisture during the hottest parts of summer.

Soil

In general, magnolias thrive in acidic soils with a pH of 5.5–6.5. However, many will also thrive in an alkaline soil (pH of 7 or higher). *Magnolia stellata*, *M. ×soulangeana*, and *M. laevifolia* are tolerant of soils with a relatively high pH. Evergreen magnolias will benefit from supplemental fertilizing with iron and nitrates.

In terms of water, magnolias in general prefer climates where there is a reasonable amount of moisture spread throughout the seasons. An annual rainfall total of 30 inches (76 cm) or more will be sufficient for growing a broad range of magnolias. In climates like those of California, Oregon, and Washington, where there is very little precipitation in summer months, and in areas where very hot and extended summer temperatures occur, supplemental irrigation will be necessary.

Most magnolias in their native habitats grow in woodlands with relatively rocky or porous soils, therefore it is these types of well-drained conditions that most will enjoy in the cultivated garden. The sweetbay magnolias (*M. virginiana* var. *australis* and *M. virginiana* var. *virginiana*), however, are an exception. In the wild, trees or thickets are often found growing in swampy areas or in standing water at the edge of ponds or lakes. As a result, in both their native settings and the garden, both varieties of the sweetbay, along with cultivars like 'Green Shadow', 'Henry Hicks', 'Mattie Mae Smith', 'Ned's Northern Belle', 'Satellite', 'Santa Rosa', and Sweet Thing 'Perry Paige' can tolerate "wet feet."

Planting

Minimal care is needed with newly planted trees. As soon as the tree is planted, it would be very beneficial to deeply water the tree or shrub. In general, deep watering should occur weekly for the first year until the magnolia

The saucer magnolia, *Magnolia ×soulangeana*, is tolerant of more alkaline soils.

is established. Mulching is also suggested. Around the base of the tree apply 2 inches (5 cm) of composted leaves or bark or triple-shredded hardwood bark mulch. It is imperative to keep the mulch away from the trunk of the tree. The mulch will hold in moisture and suppress weeds as the tree is establishing.

Magnolias are generally sold in containers, though larger trees may come balled and burlapped. Many of the planting practices that are used for magnolias would be the same practices used for a number of trees. For containerized plants, it is imperative that the congested and dense roots that you'll inevitably find in the container be loosened and teased out. Planting depth will be

Magnolias are typically sold in containers, like these *Magnolia macrophylla* pots growing at Pleasant Run Nursery in Allentown, New Jersey.

determined by the size of the root mass. The top of the root mass should be even with the top of the planting site when it is planted, though you might want to plant the magnolia slightly high since the roots will inevitably settle.

For larger balled and burlapped plants, it is critical to set the magnolia in the planting hole with the burlap intact. Balled and burlapped trees come from nurseries, where often during the process of cultivating between the rows for weed suppression, soil is inadvertently piled at the base of the plants. So when you buy a plant from the nursery it is important to pull the soil from the base of the tree and expose the root flare, the first significant set of roots appearing at the base of the trunk. Planting depth should also be in line with the existing soil level when planted. When the tree is in the planting hole cut away the top 50 percent of the burlap. The lower 50 percent can remain intact and can help stabilize the ball; it will decompose in about a year. If the top of the tree seems loose after planting, it might be necessary to stake the tree for about a year until the roots have established themselves and the tree is stable.

Pruning

As a general rule, magnolias need very little pruning. However, some selective pruning can help the aesthetic appearance of the tree or shrub. Many deciduous magnolias have vigorous shoots, known as epicormic shoots or waterspouts, that form along the stem. If these are unsightly, they can be pruned in midwinter or late summer. Other general, selective pruning can be done to open up the canopy, remove crossing branches, or to generally improve the architectural aspect of the tree.

Many cultivars and hybrids are grafted onto *Magnolia kobus* or *M. acuminata* and other species (understock). Throughout the life of the tree the understock will continue to grow and produce basal stems or shoots (suckers). It is important to be aware of this potential growth and prune away the suckers when they occur.

Many species of evergreen magnolias can be trimmed into hedges, espaliers, and topiaries. All this pruning should be done with hand pruners and not hedge shears. The hedge shears will cut many of the leaves in half and leave them unsightly. When pruning, make your cuts to a spot only slightly above the leaf. *Magnolia grandiflora*, in particular, can be manipulated into all sorts of shapes, forms, and hedging.

North American Natives

For those desiring a North American native magnolia for their landscape, there are several options that are native mostly to the eastern part of the United States. The sweetbay magnolias have a considerable range: *Magnolia virginiana* var. *virginiana* is native to North Carolina to Massachusetts along the Coastal Plain, while *M. virginiana* var. *australis* is found in the South from South Carolina south to Florida and west to Texas. There is even a population that occurs in Cuba. Both of these varieties have incredibly fragrant flowers and are extremely tolerant of wet soils.

Native North American Magnolias

Magnolia acuminata and *M. acuminata* var. *subcordata*
Magnolia fraseri
Magnolia grandiflora and cultivars
Magnolia macrophylla and *M. macrophylla* subsp. *ashei*
Magnolia tripetala
Magnolia virginiana var. *australis* and cultivars
Magnolia virginiana var. *virginiana*

The southern magnolia, *Magnolia grandiflora*, is coveted for its shiny evergreen leaves and large, white, fragrant flowers in summer. In the wild it is found along the Coastal Plain of the southeastern United States from eastern North Carolina south to central Florida and west to eastern Texas. Several species are notable for their oversized white flowers and large tropical foliage.

The aptly named bigleaf magnolia, *Magnolia macrophylla* has a native range from Ohio and Kentucky south to Georgia and west to Arkansas and Louisiana. A diminutive relative is the Ashe magnolia, *M. macrophylla* subsp. *ashei*, which has the same tropical attributes but is smaller and is restricted to the Florida Panhandle in its native habitat.

The umbrella magnolia, *Magnolia tripetala*, reaches 50 feet (15 m) tall at maturity, sports long, and has an attractive fruiting cone that turns pinkish red in autumn. It has a native range from Pennsylvania to Georgia and west to Mississippi and Arkansas.

The Fraser magnolia, *Magnolia fraseri*, has large, white, upward-facing flowers with a slight fragrance. While the leaves are not as large as those of *M. macrophylla*, *M. tripetala*, or *M. macrophylla* subsp. *ashei*, they are still quite long and provide a somewhat tropical effect in the garden. In the wild, it is found through the Southern Appalachian Mountains from Virginia to Kentucky and to Georgia and Alabama.

Pest and Diseases

Relatively speaking, magnolias suffer from very few pest and disease problems. However, there are several to be aware of depending on where you cultivate magnolias.

In many parts of the United States, the white-tailed deer can be a major pest. Deer will browse on magnolia stems, but the most significant problem occurs when deer rub against young trees. This is likely to occur in late summer or early autumn when the deer rub the velvet-like fur off their new antlers. They will rub an entire side of a young tree and can either do significant damage or kill the tree. This is best prevented by putting a wire cage around the tree. Once the tree is big enough and is not pliable enough for the deer to bend over, then the cage can be removed.

Magnolia grandiflora, here shown growing up a wall, is easily manipulated into various shapes, forms, and hedging.

Magnolia scale is a small brown scale insect with a whitish covering that exclusively attacks magnolias. At about a half inch (1 cm) in size, it is one of the largest scale insects in the United States. Cottony cushion scale, tuliptree scale, and calico scale can pose similar problems. Feeding by all of these scales reduces the vigor and health of the magnolia. Culturally, overfertilization can cause scale to be more of a problem. Scale can be remedied by several means: horticultural oils, dormant oils, and insecticidal sprays can all be employed.

Yellow poplar weevil is a beetle found throughout the eastern United States that tends to target magnolias; larvae feed on the buds and leaves of *Magnolia grandiflora* and *M. virginiana*. Another insect that also feeds on these species is the magnolia serpentine leafminer. The larvae feed on the leaves and the affected area becomes necrotic. Damage from the yellow poplar weevil may generally be superficial and not require treatment, however, if the pest population is significant, the insecticides Orthene and Sevin can be effective. The damage from the magnolia serpentine leafminer is generally cosmetic and rarely would require treatment.

A relatively new pest in parts of southern California, the polyphagous shot hole borer (or PSHB) is a relative of the ambrosia beetle and related to the tea shot hole borer. This very small beetle was found in 2014 in Los Angeles, Orange, Riverside, San Bernardino, and San Diego counties. It is a vector for three pathogenic fungi, *Fusarium*, *Graphium*, and *Sarocladium*. To date, several species that are prone to infection include *Magnolia campbellii*, *M. denudata*, *M. doltsopa*, *M. grandiflora*, *M. ×soulangeana*, and *M. sprengeri*, among others. Often, one of the first symptoms of infection is wilting from when the fungi clog the vascular system of the plant. Because they are so small, it is often hard to detect the beetle entry holes on the stems, trunk, and roots. The level of infestation will determine the overall stress to the tree and its ultimate impact. Because this pest is new, remedies and solutions have not yet been developed. Good garden practices will help prevent the spread of the fungi: clean pruning tools between usage, and be sure to remove and dispose of fallen leaves from infected trees.

In some parts of the world slugs can also pose a problem, especially when plants are young. Using an appropriate slug bait for young plants will prevent against possible defoliation.

In the southeastern United States several diseases have been reported to be problematic. Verticillium wilt can cause plants to wilt and eventually die over a period of a few years, though sometimes symptoms can be slower. Stress to trees will often exacerbate this disease. Phytophthora root rot is a root-borne disease that is characterized by wilting, dieback, and yellowing leaves. Poor drainage and too much irrigation usually contributes to Phytophthora.

During warm and humid conditions, anthracnose can develop, especially on *Magnolia grandiflora*. The primary symptoms are large brown spots on the leaves, which can contribute to premature leaf drop. In similar conditions, southern magnolias might also suffer from Phyllosticta leaf spot, which is characterized by white spots with black borders. There are several fungicides available that can be used to control anthracnose. Be sure to remove and dispose of fallen leaves from infected trees to prevent further spread.

A common disease for *Magnolia stellata* and *M. ×soulangeana* is powdery mildew.

Symptoms include powdery white patches on the leaves. Too much moisture and poor air circulation help spread this disease. Fungicides can be used as a preventative. Once the powdery mildew is established, it becomes difficult to eradicate. To alleviate issues with air circulation, try not to overplant magnolias, and thin the canopy as needed. Be careful with overhead watering, as this can also exacerbate the situation. Again, be sure to clean up fallen leaves from infected trees.

Climate Issues

In addition to pests and diseases, there are other factors that can affect the health and vigor of magnolias in the landscape. Winter burn, bark cracking, frost cracking, and sunscald are problems caused by changes in the weather that can cause physiological damage to magnolias.

WINTER BURN

Winter burn is a problem for both evergreen and semi-evergreen magnolias. It generally happens to the plants and leaves that are most exposed to the wind and direct sun. During winter, when the ground is frozen, magnolias will continue to transpire small amounts of water. When the tree is unable to replace the transpired water from the frozen ground, leaves can burn and dessicate resulting in edges of leaves being burned, scorched, and possibly defoliating. However, the damage is usually superficial.

Winter burn can be avoided by positioning evergreen and semi-evergreen magnolias in areas where they are somewhat shaded during the winter. This will also protect them from wind. Planting them in courtyards will also provide protection. At Scott Arboretum, *Magnolia grandiflora* 'Hasse' and *Magnolia virginiana* var. *australis* 'Santa Rosa' both benefit from the protection of courtyard walls. If walls are not available to offer protection, you can build a simple frame with four posts and burlap to provide protection in the winter (though this method shrouds some of the winter display of the evergreens). Another option is to select more cold-hardy cultivars such as *Magnolia grandiflora* 'Pocono', 'D. D. Blanchard', or 'Edith Bogue'.

BARK CRACKING, FROST CRACKING, AND SUNSCALD

Warm temperatures heading into autumn can lead to bark cracking on some magnolias—yellow magnolias, in particular, are susceptible to this. Most magnolias have thin bark; with warm temperatures or over-fertilization heading into autumn and winter, some magnolias may not harden properly and then cold temperatures can result in bark cracking. A few years back at Scott Arboretum we had three young *Magnolia* 'Judy Zuk' trees all get severe bark cracking to the point where one had to be removed.

Frost cracking causes a vertical crack on the side of the trunk and is caused by wounds, root injury, or poor pruning. Extreme temperature fluctuations are ideal conditions for frost cracks to develop.

Sunscald can also result from extreme temperature fluctuations. During winter months, the cambium on bark exposed to the sun can reach 70°F (21°C) or higher, even when the outside temperatures might be freezing or lower. The cold exposure to the warm cambium can result in "burned" areas that lead to sunken or discolored bark that might split open at a later date.

Propagation

For home gardeners, the usual methods of propagating magnolia are from seed or cuttings. Using grafting techniques is another way, like cuttings, to vegetatively propagate a new plant. Like cuttings, this will ensure that the exact cultivar, hybrid, or species is being replicated. Chip-budding and winter and summer grafting techniques can be employed to vegetatively propagate magnolias, however these methods are often more easily executed in commercial or large-scale operations.

Recently grafted plants of 'Eric Savill', 'Golden Gift', 'Honey Liz', 'Hattie Carthan', and 'Stephens Creek'.

First year grafts in the spring.

Close-up of a first year graft.

Seedling production of assorted magnolias.

SEED

Many magnolias are easy to grow from seed, and pretty much any species can be grown this way. Seeds from uncontrolled hybrids can be harvested and germinated. These would be seeds collected from any magnolia tree that was likely pollinated by a neighboring tree. Seeds can also be harvested from trees where controlled crosses have been made. For example, *Magnolia* 'Ann' was a controlled hybrid, conducted by Francis deVos at the US National Arboretum, between *M. liliiflora* 'Nigra' and *M. stellata* 'Rosea'. The seed was harvested from this resulting cross, germinated, and then the plants were grown on until they began to flower. From these one seedling was selected and named 'Ann'. A great many new cultivars are the results of selection of seedlings from controlled hybridization.

Magnolia 'Ann', the result of a cross between *M. liliiflora* 'Nigra' and *M. stellata* 'Rosea'.

As the aggregate of follicles (or fruit) matures seeds will begin to protrude from the carpels as they split open. At this point the individual seed can be collected or the entire cone can be collected and the seed harvested from that. At Scott Arboretum, we collected the seed as soon as it appeared ripe. We put the seed in bucket of warm water and within a couple days the shiny red seed coat has been compromised and the seed can be separated from the seed coat. By putting them in a bucket of water you can harvest only the viable seed. Any non-viable seed will float and the viable seeds will sink to the bottom of the bucket. It is important to keep magnolia seed fresh and moist, so we stored our seed in slightly milled peat or sphagnum or in finely milled vermiculite. The seeds are then placed in the refrigerator until it is time to sow them.

Seeds can be sown in autumn or spring. They can be planted in containers or a low flat (shallow container). A commercial potting soil can be used, though a fine composted material will be sufficient as well. If planted in autumn, seedlings can stay outside during winter in a cold frame protected with wire mesh to keep out any animals that might get at them. This cold treatment will help with the germination process in spring. The seed can also be stored in the refrigerator for two months and then sown in spring for similar results. If exposed to temperatures of 70°F (21°C) and by keeping the planting medium moist, germination should occur in 30 to 40 days.

CUTTINGS

Vegetative cuttings can be taken from many of the deciduous and evergreen species of magnolias. For most deciduous species, a softwood cutting would be suggested. The timing for taking the cutting depends on where you are located, but this should generally happen in midspring. They should be about 3–6 inches (8–15 cm) long, and should be taken from the current season's growth. New growth is somewhere in between firm and pliable, which makes it ideal.

An assortment of rooted magnolia cuttings.

Rooted cuttings of evergreen species.

Evergreen hardwood cutting propagation.

For evergreen species such as *Magnolia grandiflora*, a similar cutting can be taken in mid- to late summer when the cuttings are more "ripe." These are called semi-ripe cuttings. Since these cuttings may not root until autumn, they should probably stay in their pots until the subsequent spring and then be potted up. Cuttings should be made right below a leaf node. The upper leaves can be cut in half. A rooting hormone or rooting powder can be applied to the wound below the node to help initiate root formation. A rooting hormone with between 0.3 to 0.7 iba (indolebutyric acid) is suggested. The cut surface of the cutting is simply stuck in the powder. The cuttings can then be put in a pot with a finely milled potting soil. The cuttings can be misted and a clear polyethylene bag put over the pot to created a greenhouse effect until the cuttings are rooted. Once a strong root system develops the individual cuttings taken in May can be potted into individual pots.

WHERE TO BUY

AUSTRALIA
Yamina Rare Plants
82 David Hill Road
Monbulk, Victoria 3793
www.yaminarareplants.com.au

CANADA
The Honey Tree
24202 Hwy 2
Norboro, Prince Edward Island COB 1MO
www.thehoneytreenursery.com

GERMANY
Lunaplant.de
Mühlstr. 7
D-65779 Kelkheim
www.lunaplant.de

NETHERLANDS
Magnoliastore
Horsterdijk 103
5973 PM Lottum
www.magnoliastore.com

NEW ZEALAND
Magnolia Grove
Waitara, Taranaki
www.magnoligrove.co.nz

Wairere Nursery
826 Gordonton Road
RD 1, Hamilton
www.wairere.co.nz

POLAND
Zymon Ornamental Nursery
Tłokinia Wielka 34
62-860 Opatówek
www.zymon.pl

SWITZERLAND
Eisenhut Nursery
CH-6575 San Nazzaro
www.eisenhut.ch

UNITED KINGDOM
BlueBell Arboretum and Nursery
Annwell Lane
Simsby
Ashby de la Zouch
Leicestershire LE65 2TA
England
www.bluebellnursery.com

Burncoose Nurseries
Gwennap
Redruth
Cornwall TR16 6BJ
England
www.burncoose.co.uk

Crug Farm Plants
Griffith's Crossing
Caernarfon
Gwynedd LL55 1TU
Wales
www.crug-farm.co.uk

Duchy of Cornwall Nursery
Cott Road
Lostwithiel
Cornwall PL22 0HW
England
www.duchyofcornwallnursery.co.uk

Hillier Nurseries
Ampfield House
Ampfield
Romsey
Hampshire SO51 9PA
England
www.hillier.co.uk

Junker's Nursery
Higher Cobhay
Milverton
Somerset TA4 1NJ
England
www.junker.co.uk

Kevin Hughes Plants
Middle Woodford
Wiltshire SP4 6NT
England
www.kevinsplants.co.uk

Mallet Court Nursery
Marshway
Curry Mallet
Taunton TA3 6SZ
England
www.malletcourt.co.uk

Pan-Global Plants
The Walled Garden
Frampton-on-Severn
Frampton Court
Gloucestershire GL2 7EX
England
www.panglobalplants.com

Wisley Plant Centre
RHS Garden Wisley
Woking
Surrey GU23 6QB
England
www.rhs.org

UNITED STATES

Broken Arrow Nursery
13 Broken Arrow Road
Hamden, Connecticut 06518
www.brokenarrownursery.com

Camellia Forest Nursery
620 N. Carolina Hwy 54 W
Chapel Hill, North Carolina 27516
www.camforest.com

Cistus Nursery
22711 NW Gillihan Road
Portland, Oregon 97231
www.cistus.com

Forest Farm Nursery
14643 Watergap Road
Williams, Oregon 97544
www.forestfarm.com

Gossler Farms Nursery
1200 Weaver Road
Springfield, Oregon 97478
www.gosslerfarms.com

Greer Gardens
1280 Good Pasture Island Road
Eugene, Oregon 97401
www.greergardens.com

Rare Find Nursery
957 Patterson Road
Jackson, New Jersey 08527
www.rarefindnursery.com

Song Sparrow Nursery
13101 E. Rye Road
Avalon, Wisconsin 53505
www.songsparrow.com

Top Tropicals
13890 Orange River Boulevard
Ft Myers, Florida 33905
www.toptropicals.com

Whitman Farms
3995 Gibson Road NW
Salem, Oregon 97304
www.whitmanfarms.com

Woodlander's Inc.
1128 Colleton Avenue
Aiken, South Carolina 29801
www.woodlanders.net

WHERE TO SEE

AUSTRALIA
Royal Botanic Gardens, Melbourne
Birdwood Avenue
South Yarra, Victoria 3141
www.rbg.vic.gov.au

BELGIUM
Arboretum Bokrijk
Provinciaal Domein Bokrijk
B-3600 Bokrijk
www.bokrijk.be

Arboretum Kalmthout
Heuvel 8
2920 Kalmthout
www.arboretumkalmthout.be

Arboretum Wespelaar
Grote Baan 63
B-3150 Haacht-Wespelaar
www.arboretumwespelaar.be

CANADA
Royal Botanic Gardens, Hamilton
680 Plains Road W
Burlington, Ontario L7T 4H4
www.rbg.ca

University of British Colombia Botanical Garden
6804 Marine Drive SW
Vancouver, British Columbia V6T 1Z4
www.botanicalgarden.ubc.ca

VanDusen Botanical Garden
5251 Oak Street
Vancouver, British Columbia V6M 4H1
www.vandusen.org

CHINA
South China Botanical Garden
1190 Tianyuan Road
Tianhe, Guangzhou
Guangdong
www.scib.ac.cn

COLOMBIA
Jardín Botánico José Celestino Mutis
Avenida 63 #N o. 68–95
Bogota
www.jbb.gov.co

FRANCE
Arboretum des Grandes Bruyères
45450 Ingrannes
www.arboretumdesgrandesbruyeres.fr

IRELAND
National Botanic Gardens, Glasnevin
Glasnevin
Dublin 9
www.botanicgardens.ie

ITALY
Giardini Botanici Villa Taranto
Via Vittorio Veneto, 111
28922 Verbania, Piemonte
www.villataranto.it.en

NETHERLANDS
Arboretum Trompenburg
Honingerdijk 86
3062 NX Rotterdam
www.trompenburg.nl

NEW ZEALAND
Aukland Botanic Gardens
102 Hill Road
Aukland 2105
www.auklandbotanicgardens.co.nz

Christchurch Botanic Gardens
Christchurch Central
Christchurch 8013
www.gardens.org.nz

Dunedin Botanic Garden
North Dunedin
Dunedin 9016
www.dunedinbotanicgarden.co.nz

SOUTH KOREA
Chollipo Arboretum
875 Uihang-ri
Sowon-myeon, Taean-gun
Chungchungnam-do
www.taekids.com

UNITED KINGDOM
Bodnant Garden
National Collection of Magnolias
Tal-y-cafn, Colwyn Bay
Clwyd LL28 5RE
Wales
www.nationaltrust.org

Borde Hill Gardens
Borde Hill Lane
Haywards Heath, West Sussex RH16 1XP
England
www.bordehill.co.uk

Caerhays Castle
National Collection of Magnolias
Gorran
Saint Austell PL26 6LY
www.caerhays.com

Glendurgan Garden
Glendurgan, Falmouth
Cornwall TR11 5JZ
England
www.nationaltrust.org.uk

Royal Botanic Garden Edinburgh
Arboretum Place
Edinburgh EH3 5NZ
Scotland
www.rbge.uk

Royal Botanic Gardens, Kew
Kew, Richmond
Surrey TW9 3AB
England
www.kew.org

Royal Horticultural Society, Rosemoor
Devon
www.rhs.org.uk/gardens/rosemoor

Royal Horticultural Society, Wisley
Wisley Lane, Wisley
Woking GU23 6QB
England
www.rhs.org.uk

The Savill and Valley Gardens, Windsor Great Park
Windsor, Berkshire SL4 2HT
England
www.theroyallandscape.co.uk

Sir Harold Hillier Gardens and Arboretum
Jermyns Lane, Ampfield
Romsey
Hampshire SO51 0QA
England
www.hilliergardens.org.uk

Trewithen Gardens and Nursery
Grampound Road
Truro
Cornwall TR2 4DD
England
www.trewithengardens.co.uk

Wakehurst Place
Ardingly
Haywards Heath
Sussex RH17 6TN
England
www.kew.org

Westonbirt, The National Arboretum
Westonbirt
Tetbury
Gloucestershire GL8 8QS
England
www.westonbirtarboretum.com

UNITED STATES

Atlanta Botanical Garden
1345 Piedmont Avenue NE
Atlanta, Georgia 30309
www.atlantabg.org

Bartlett Tree Research Laboratories and Arboretum
13768 Hamilton Road
Charlotte, North Carolina 28278
www.bartlett.com/bartlett-tree-research

Brooklyn Botanic Garden
990 Washington Avenue
Brooklyn, New York 11225
www.bbg.org

Chicago Botanic Garden
1000 Lake Cook Road
Glencoe, Illinois 60022
www.chicagobotanic.org

Green Bay Botanical Garden
2600 Larsen Road
Green Bay, Wisconsin 54303
www.gbbg.org

Hoyt Arboretum
4000 SW Fairview Boulevard
Portland, Oregon 97221
www.hoytarboretum.org

Huntington Botanical Garden
1151 Oxford Road
San Marino, California 91108
www.huntington.org

JC Raulston Arboretum
4415 Beryl Road
Raleigh, North Carolina 27606
www.jcra.ncsu.edu

Lewis Ginter Botanical Garden
1800 Lakeside Avenue
Henrico, Virginia 23228
www.lewisginter.org

Meredith College
3800 Hillsborough Street
Raleigh, North Carolina 27607
www.meredith.edu

Moore Farms Botanical Garden
100 New Zion Road
Lake City, South Carolina 29560
www.moorefarmsbg.org

Morris Arboretum at the University of Pennsylvania
100 E Northwestern Avenue
Philadelphia, Pennsylvania 19118
www.morrisarboretum.org

Morton Arboretum
4100 IL-53
Lisle, Illinois 60532
www.mortonarb.org

New York Botanical Garden
2900 Southern Boulevard
Bronx, New York 10458
www.nybg.org

Powell Gardens
1609 NW US Hwy 50
Kingsville, Missouri 64061
www.powellgardens.org

Quarryhill Botanical Garden
12841 Hwy 12
Glen Ellen, California 95442
www.quarryhillbg.org

San Francisco Botanical Garden
1199 9th Avenue
San Francisco, California 94122
www.sfbotanicalgarden.org

Scott Arboretum of Swarthmore College
500 College Avenue
Swarthmore, Pennsylvania 19081
www.scottarboretum.org

South Carolina Botanical Garden
150 Discovery Lane
Clemson, South Carolina 29631
www.clemson.edu

Spartanburg Community College
107 Community College Drive
Spartanburg, South Carolina 29303
www.sccsc.edu

University of California Botanical Garden at Berkeley
200 Centennial Drive
Berkeley, California 94720
www.botanicalgarden.berkeley.edu

University of Washington Botanic Gardens
3501 NE 41st Street
Seattle, Washington 98105
www.depts.washington.edu/uwbg

US National Arboretum
3501 New York Avenue E
Washington, DC 20002
www.usna.usda.gov

FOR MORE INFORMATION

BOOKS

Barrett, Rosemary, and Hughes, Derek. 2002. *Magnolias*. Richmond Hill, Ontario: Firefly Books.

Callaway, Dorothy J. 1994. *The World of Magnolias*. Portland, Oregon: Timber Press.

Dirr, Michael A. 2009. *Manual of Woody Landscape Plants: Their Identification, Ornamental Characteristics, Culture, Propagation and Uses*. Champaign, Illinois: Stipes Publishing.

Gardiner, Jim. 2000. *Magnolias: A Gardener's Guide*. Portland, Oregon: Timber Press.

Oozeerally, Barbara, Jim Gardiner, and Stephen A. Spongberg 2014. *Magnolias in Art and Cultivation*. Chicago, Illinois: The University of Chicago Press.

Rankin, Graham. 1999. *Magnolias: A Hamlyn Care Manual*. Hamlyn.

ORGANIZATIONS

Arboretum Wespelaar
www.arboretumwespelaar.be

Magnolia Society International
www.magnolisociety.org

Royal Horticultural Society Rhododendron, Camellia, and Magnolia Group
www.rhodogroup-rhs.org

HARDINESS ZONE TEMPERATURES

USDA ZONES & CORRESPONDING TEMPERATURES

Temp °F			Zone	Temp °C		
−60	to	−55	1a	−51	to	−48
−55	to	−50	1b	−48	to	−46
−50	to	−45	2a	−46	to	−43
−45	to	−40	2b	−43	to	−40
−40	to	−35	3a	−40	to	−37
−35	to	−30	3b	−37	to	−34
−30	to	−25	4a	−34	to	−32
−25	to	−20	4b	−32	to	−29
−20	to	−15	5a	−29	to	−26
−15	to	−10	5b	−26	to	−23
−10	to	−5	6a	−23	to	−21
−5	to	0	6b	−21	to	−18
0	to	5	7a	−18	to	−15
5	to	10	7b	−15	to	−12
10	to	15	8a	−12	to	−9
15	to	20	8b	−9	to	−7
20	to	25	9a	−7	to	−4
25	to	30	9b	−4	to	−1
30	to	35	10a	−1	to	2
35	to	40	10b	2	to	4
40	to	45	11a	4	to	7
45	to	50	11b	7	to	10
50	to	55	12a	10	to	13
55	to	60	12b	13	to	16
60	to	65	13a	16	to	18
65	to	70	13b	18	to	21

FIND HARDINESS MAPS ON THE INTERNET.
United States *http://www.usna.usda.gov/Hardzone/ushzmap.html*
Canada *http://www.planthardiness.gc.ca/* or *http://atlas.nrcan.gc.ca/site/
english/maps/environment/forest/forestcanada/planthardi*
Europe *http://www.gardenweb.com/zones/europe/* or *http://www.uk.garden
web.com/forums/zones/hze.html*

ACKNOWLEDGMENTS

I want to thank both my parents for their lifelong inspiration. My mother, Judy Bunting, from an early age inspired me and fueled my passion to become a gardener, and my father, Frank Bunting, was a passionate writer. He would wait until after I went to bed and then write into the wee hours of the night. He was a great example for me.

Over the last several years I have been very fortunate to be involved on the board of directors of the Magnolia Society International. This group of magnoliaphiles has helped and inspired me on many levels as I researched and wrote this book.

Other colleagues I would like to thank include: James Adams, Anthony Aiello, Jared Barnes, Andrew Bell, Dan Billman, Timothy Boland, Carol Bordelon, Dorothy Callaway, Koen Camelbeke, Paul Cappiello, Christopher Carley, Robin Carlson, Chris Carmichael, Joshua Coceano, Christophe Crock, Patrick Cullina, William Cullina, Michael Dirr, Michael Dosman, Beth Edward, Erland Ejder, Richard Figlar, Thomas Fischer, James Gardiner, John Grimshaw, Ethan Guthrie, Eric Hammond, Edward Hasselkus, Richard Hawke, Richard Hesselein, Daniel Hinkley, Vance Hooper, Pavel Janik, Lennarth Jonsson, Abbie Jury, Mark Jury, Daryl Kobesky, Dennis Ledvina, Gary Keim, Panayoti Kelaidis, Kunso Kim, Roy Klehm, John Kuhlman, Gary Knox, Mark Krautmann, Larry Langford, Rick Lewandowski, Matt Lobdell, Don Mahoney, Kathy Musial, Martin Nicholson, Greg Paige, David Parks, Kevin Parris, Ronald Rabideau, Todd Rounsaville, Claire Sawyers, Aaron Schettler, Scott Aroberetum of Swarthmore College, Ian Simpkins, Willam Smith, Song Sparrow Nursery, Fred Spicer, Philippe de Spoelberch, Lisa Strovinsky, Raymond Sutton, Timothy Thibault, William Thomas, Eve Thyrum, John Tobe, Charles Tubesing, Vladimir Tushin, Mark Weathington, Adam Wheeler, and Carrie Wiles.

PHOTO CREDITS

ARBORETUM WESPELAAR pages 4–5, 9 (left), 21 (right), 22, 24 (right), 28 (top), 39 (right), 41 (right), 46–47, 57 (left), 62, 69, 71, 78, 80, 89, 90, 97, 99 (right), 109, 112, 128, 129, 130, 141, 145, 151, 153 (left), 154, 164, 165, 176, 177, 189, 191, 193, 194, 198–199, 211

CAMELLIA FOREST NURSERY page 86

PAUL CAPPIELLO pages 14, 25

RICHARD FIGLAR pages 2–3, 9 (right), 11, 26 (bottom), 27 (left), 44–45, 48–49, 68, 91, 119, 134, 139, 144, 158, 175, 179, 184

ETHAN GUTHRIE pages 208, 209, 210, 212, 213

RICHARD HESSELEIN pages 21 (left), 94–95, 146, 160, 188

VANCE HOOPER page 73

JC RAULSTON ARBORETUM pages 12–13, 23 (top right), 27 (right), 30, 42–43, 60, 66 (right), 70, 79, 81, 82, 101, 108, 113, 117, 118, 122, 142, 152, 153 (right), 163, 171

ABBIE JURY page 111

MARK JURY pages 61 (left), 88, 123

ROY KLEHM, SONGSPARROW.COM page 110

GARY KNOX pages 26 (top), 77, 102, 116

DARYL KOBESKY 28 (bottom), 40 (bottom), 103, 182, 183

JOHN KUHLMAN page 143

DENNIS LEDVINA pages 54–55, 58, 64, 75, 87, 147, 149, 173

KEVIN PARRIS pages 37, 72, 100, 104, 106

RONALD RABIDEAU pages 57 (right), 185

AARON SCHETTLER pages 17, 29, 39 (left), 196

THE SCOTT ARBORETUM OF SWARTHMORE COLLEGE pages 23 (left), 35 (top), 83, 85, 105, 114–115, 121, 166, 186

WILLIAM SMITH page 98

LISA STROVINSKY pages 10, 16, 32, 34 (top), 63, 66 (left), 67, 92, 96, 99 (left), 107, 108 (right), 125, 131, 135, 136, 137, 168, 169, 172, 174 (top), 181, 190, 197

ADAM WHEELER pages 35 (bottom), 38, 56, 59, 132, 174 (bottom), 203 (right)

All other photos by the author.

INDEX

ABOUT THE AUTHOR

ANDREW BUNTING is assistant director of the garden and director of collections at Chicago Botanic Garden in Glencoe, Illinois. Prior to coming to the Chicago Botanic Garden he worked at Scott Arboretum of Swarthmore College in Swarthmore, Pennsylvania, for 25 years. There as curator he helped build a national collection of magnolias recognized by the North American Plant Collections Consortium. He is on the board of directors for the Magnolia Society International and served two terms as president. With the Magnolia Society he has traveled to South Korea, Colombia, Poland, Italy, and throughout the United States looking at magnolias. He has lectured extensively on magnolias and written articles for *Arnoldia*, *Organic Gardening Magazine*, *The American Gardener*, and the *Magnolia Society Journal*, and appeared on the *Martha Stewart Living Show* to discuss magnolias.

©ROBIN CARLSON

Front cover: *Magnolia sargentiana*
Spine: *Magnolia laevifolia* 'Michelle'
Title page: *Magnolia* 'Sweetheart'
Contents page: *Magnolia* 'Wim Rutten'

The authors and publisher make reasonable efforts to ascertain the rights
status of all third-party works. Any corrections should be sent to the attention of the publisher.

Published in 2016 by Timber Press, Inc.
The Haseltine Building
133 S.W. Second Avenue, Suite 450
Portland, Oregon 97204-3527
timberpress.com

Printed in China

For details on other Timber Press books and to sign up for our newsletters,
please visit timberpress.com.

Library of Congress Cataloging-in-Publication Data

NAMES: Bunting, Andrew, author.
TITLE: The plant lover's guide to magnolias / Andrew Bunting.
DESCRIPTION: Portland, Oregon: Timber Press, 2016. | Includes index.
IDENTIFIERS: LCCN 2015036495 | ISBN 9781604695786
SUBJECTS: LCSH: Magnolias.
CLASSIFICATION: LCC SB413.M34 B86 2016 | DDC 635.9/77322—dc23 LC
    record available at http://lccn.loc.gov/2015036495

A catalog record for this book is also available from the British Library.
Mention of trademark, proprietary product, or vendor does not constitute
a guarantee or warranty of the product by the publisher or author and does
not imply its approval to the exclusion of other products or vendors.

Series design by Laken Wright
Cover design by Kristi Pfeffer